NICARAGUA
AT THE FOOT
OF THE VOLCANO

NICARAGUA
AT THE FOOT
OF THE VOLCANO

Translated from Dutch by Scott Rollins

MAARTEN ROEST

NICARAGUA. AT THE FOOT OF THE VOLCANO

iUniverse books may be ordered through booksellers or by contacting:

iUniverse
1663 Liberty Drive
Bloomington, IN 47403
www.iuniverse.com
1-800-Authors (1-800-288-4677)

Cover design © Omar Iglesias
Cover picture © Maarten Roest
Picture author © Giulio Napolitano

ISBN: 978-1-4917-7350-5 (sc)
ISBN: 978-1-4917-7351-2 (e)

Print information available on the last page.

iUniverse rev. date: 11/13/2015

Difícil es y duro el luchar contra el Olimpo acuoso de las ranas
It is a hard and difficult fight against the watery Olympus of the frogs

Carlos Martínez Rivas

CONTENTS

THE QUEEN OF THE LAKE

The winds of January scurry across the lake. Under a cloudless sky, the two volcanoes rise clearly from the waters. Only above Concepción hangs a small cloud, like a cap just above the mouth of its crater. Exposed, the Madera bathes in the midday sun.

The boat departs at three thirty. I have bought a ticket and taken a seat at one of the little eateries in front of the pier. Time enough for a midday meal. I order rice and beans, grilled chicken and fried plantain with a Victoria, one of Nicaragua's finest beers.

San Jorge is a two hour drive south of Managua. You take a left near the little white church in the middle of the village and then the first main road to the right. You drive between twin towers that resemble castle turrets, except they do not have steeples and are made of concrete. There's a ticket window in the left tower and the fares are painted on the right one. Fares for busses, cars and motorcycles. A toll will probably have to be paid here during Easter, when it's at the height of summer and the beaches of San Jorge are packed. The road ends at the pier a few hundred meters past the towers. The entrance is blocked by an iron gate. On either side of the pier run long stretches of sandy beach. There are women along the waterline with washboards on wooden stakes doing the laundry and a couple of kids who dare to venture out into the surf.

A port official opens the gate for a truck, that drives onto the pier with its freight. The official closes the gate again behind the truck. Passengers have to wait. A few families have already taken up positions. Mothers holding their children's hands, grannies sheltering from the sun under an umbrella, boys sitting on sports bags packed to the gills.

A couple of tables away from mine two women really seem to be enjoying themselves. There's a bottle of rum, two glasses of coke and a bowl with ice in front of them. One of the women asks the man walking past with a crate of Pepsi on his shoulder, if he would like to have a drink with them. When she sees me looking at them, the other one calls out:

"Come and join us!"

I lift my bottle of beer in the air and gesture that I am fine where I am.

I gaze out over what - to the naked eye – seems an endless expanse of lake water. The Concepción is an hour away by ferry. Even further, on the opposite shore, must be the hills of Chontales.

The stiff wind blows clouds of dust across the outdoor cafe. I put a hand in front of my eyes. The wind blows a great deal in Nicaragua, just as it did over a year ago the first time I came. The thing that first caught my attention though when I stepped out of the plane at the airport from a cold Europe, was the smell. And the heat. It feels like you are walking into a greenhouse. It has the same kind of odor and naturally, it is just as hot.

The image in my mind at the time of my first arrival was only vague at best. A tropical country that had undergone a revolution. I knew what Daniel Ortega looked like, thick glasses and moustache under a soft army cap. I did not exactly warm to the image he projected. There was something courageous about the Sandinista struggle, but also something sad, something impossible. The Sandinistas had just lost the elections for a second time when I first came. The people were complaining. Everything was getting more expensive, electricity, telephone, gas. How were you supposed to come up with your children's school tuition? And what if they had to go to the hospital? Things used to be different, things used to be taken care of. And the streets were not as unsafe either. But indeed, in today's Nicaragua nobody does anything for the poor anymore. People steal out of desperation.

Nicaragua had long since stopped being the 'violently dear Nicaragua' of the Argentine author Julio Cortázar, from whose pen one of the most passionate declarations of love for the Sandinista revolution had flowed. In Cortázar's new Nicaragua the 'smile of freedom' was abroad everywhere you looked, as well as the 'the freedom of the smile.' Anyone arriving at Managua airport felt a different kind of breeze than this warm wind now blowing dust into my face: "The wind of freedom was your pilot, and the compass of the people indicated north," Cortázar wrote to the traveler, and to he who doubted: "No, you have not mistaken the airport: come further, you are in Nicaragua."

One year ago, when I walked off the airport under an enormous sign that read: WELCOME TO THE REPUBLIC OF NICARAGUA, I did not feel a wind of freedom blowing through my hair, nor did I expect anyone to point out where north was. After all, revolutionary nostalgia had not been my reason for coming here. In July 1979, when the Sandinistas ousted the dictator from power, I still had not reached my twelfth birthday. As far I was concerned, the only real news from Latin America in those days was coming from Argentina, where the Dutch national soccer team had lost in the finals of the World Cup the previous year. And, can you be a revolutionary, if you are born in 1967, two months before the ignominious death of that embodiment of the New Man, Che Guevara? Hadn't the revolution been dead and buried with his passing?

After the revolution of 1979 it was not a smile that was abroad in Nicaragua, but the ghost of a 'second Cuba', so the United States feared. This was supposed to be the country of land reform, where people were taught to read and write, the country of the 'democratization of culture', of popular theater, the poetry workshops and the primitive painting, the land of peasant masses, of God for the people, where Christians and

Marxists strove together for a just society, the land where an all-embracing revolution had taken place, which the poet priest Ernesto Cardenal had summarized as follows: "The revolution is the most prominent work of art our people have produced."

I was shocked at what I saw. The shacks of corrugated iron sheets and rusting zinc roofs. The children at the traffic lights. Their ragged clothes, filthy feet and their faces, that looked like they were covered with soot by the stinking exhaust fumes of the busses. For the first time I saw poverty up close.

But I did see lots of smiles. In doorways, at crossroads, at bus stops. Whether they were smiles of freedom, I could not tell. One month after my arrival, I discovered you grow accustomed to the sight of poverty. Just like you do to rice and beans, with grilled chicken and fried plantain. And the heat. You practically don't notice the greenhouse odor anymore after descending the aircraft steps.

A month later I was also on Tiscapa hill for the first time, the highest point within the Managua city limits. A paradoxical place. Here stands Ernesto Cardenal's iron statue of the freedom fighter Sandino. Like a gigantic ode to liberty it looms above the capital city. Not much farther on is Somoza's 'bunker', the place where his National Guard are supposed to have carried out their most cruel acts of torture.

From the hilltop there is a panoramic view of Managua, "standing amid the ruins, beautiful in its fallow land", as Cortázar wrote at the beginning of the 1980s. He saw a city in ruins. The funds received to rebuild the city after the earthquake of 1972 had largely disappeared into Somoza's pockets and during the war years of the nineteen eighties, there were other things on people's minds than restoring the devastated city.

The rubble has been cleared away after the peace of 1990. The few buildings that still remained standing after the earthquake have now gotten neighbors. Not far from the white tower of the Bank of America an apartment complex was built with blue plate-glass windows. In the shade of the Intercontinental Hotel, that oblong pyramid at the foot of Tiscapa hill, a shopping mall has risen. Nonetheless, the city is more reminiscent of some huge garden village. You have to look hard to find any residential housing among the palm and banana trees along the banks of Xolotlán, the lake at Managua. When you drive down from the hill open fields extend before your eyes. This used to be the city center, now there are only a few ruins. And it should come as no surprise to see a cow grazing.

The statue is still there. Militantly thrusting its rifle into the air. The blue iron must have lost some paint since the time when one sympathizer after another had their picture taken in front of this heroic *guerrillero,* drawn by the cry of freedom that he, with his chin held proudly aloft, seems to hurl to the skies. What has become of all these pictures?

Further on, behind the National Palace and the old cathedral without a roof, is Managua's boulevard. Imagine an avenue in the shade of waving palm trees, with bustling sidewalk cafes on one side and the beach sloping downward on the other, and Managua could very well resemble an elegant city on the lakeshore. There are indeed palm trees along the boulevard, but the promenade arching over the waterfront affords scanty access to the water. The city "turns its back on the lake," wrote Sergio Ramírez, one of Nicaruaga's most prominent novelists and vice-president during the Sandinista government, "to relieve itself in its waters and turn it into a cesspit". If there is an onshore breeze, the stench of raw sewage is unbearable.

Under the promenade, meters below, are blocks of concrete, rubble and garbage. The turbulent water pounds into it, but the concrete is hard and the water ricochets back. "The lake is a mirage," according to Ramírez, and Managua – "the mocked bride of Xolotlán" – an enemy to its surroundings and nature, that avenges itself, like with the earthquake in 1972.

When Julio Cortázar passed away in 1984, he took his promised Nicaragua unmoved with him to his grave. Later on the face of that dear country began showing grimaces. Censorship was imposed. The army abused its power. What would Cortázar think of the Sandinista leaders after their defeat in the 1990 elections, when they robbed the state of businesses, land and houses, an act of theft that was named after the game played by children using a doll filled with candy which they hit with a stick and break grabbing everything in a free for all: the *piñata*. A single word, a telling description of the unmasking of the people's revolution. One image, the battered head of a doll. The smile had disappeared.

These days Cortázar's writings about Nicaragua read like romanticized tributes to utopia. But that is in hindsight, now that everything has come to an end. The Berlin Wall no longer exists, the Cold War is relegated to history books and Nicaragua has lost its revolution. The small country, that once seemed so great in its struggle, vanished from the thoughts of world class authors and ceased to attract the attention of the makers of world news.

In Managua, you are warned from all sides. The most often heard piece of advice: don't go out on the street for no good reason. Take a taxi or drive your own car. Lock the doors, close the windows and put on the air-conditioning. You have to be especially careful at traffic lights with all those kids around. As far as that goes traffic circles are a godsend: no traffic lights. Take Metrocentro, for example. At night, isn't a treat to see the water illuminated by the red, green, blue and yellow lights gushing from the fountains in the center of the traffic circle? The enormous Victoria beer ad on the side of the road is now joined by a huge Coca Cola billboard. A new McDonald's has opened its doors. Unmistakable signs of progress. People were rolling up their sleeves in Nicaragua again. Weren't there fewer potholes in the roads? Wasn't the economy on a roll? And hadn't they got rid of the 30,000 percent inflation rampant under the Sandinistas?

In Nicaragua I got to know a people of talkers. I heard stories about now and the past, a wistful memory alongside tales of hard feelings, joy interchanged with desperation, nostalgia along with relief. As a rule, not stories I was after for the news stories I was writing about Central America. Not world news or all-embracing expositions. Instead, they could be a detail that cleared up the confusing historical accounts from the colonial era or the bloody decade of the eighties. A casual remark that shone light on the contrasts between the descendants of the Spaniards on the one hand and those of the Native Americans or the blacks on the Caribbean coast on the other. Sometimes it was the look in someone's eye that brought to life the theoretical views concerning the tortured existence of the *mestizos*.

Once the port official reopens the gate, the passengers walk down the pier towards the ferry. Fine drops of water, sprayed by the wind, fall on my face. The pier ends at a jetty of dark blocks of stone behind which the *Reina del Lago* – the Queen of the Lake – is moored beyond the reach of the waves. Her green hull looks as though it could easily fit into one of the high waves, smashing into smithereens on the blocks of stone. But I am told there have never been any accidents, and the Reina always sails, waves or no waves.

On the stroke of three-thirty the hawsers are cast off and the little ship grumbles into the turbulent water. The lake is at its roughest along the coast at San Jorge. The ship rises and falls with a thud, lurching from left to right and plowing resolutely ahead. Water splashes over the starboard side. A woman is hit full blast. She laughs. Her fellow passengers laugh too. Everyone goes on with their chatter. My neighbor assures me things could be much worse. He closes his eyes to have a snooze.

The Reina sets course for Moyogalpa at the foot of the Concepción. It is the taller of the two volcanoes. The most conical one in Nicaragua, they say on the island. As we approach, the mountain appears to get bigger and bigger. Trees cover the bottom half, then the slope is permeated with deep gullies, that lead up to the pointed summit. The small cap of cloud has blown away. The mouth of the volcano now lies like jaws wide open to the sky. In recent years Concepción has become active again.

In contrast, the Madera has been silent for centuries. A lagoon has formed in its wide crater. The blunt peak in the distance, sheathed in a blanket of dense tropical forest, looks benign.

According to legend, the first inhabitants of Ometepe were the Chorotega Indians, who had fled Mexico, where they had groaned under the yoke of the Olmecs. They decided to seek a place to settle elsewhere and consulted their gods, who spoke of the Promised Land that lay to the South. They were not to settle until they had come to a fresh water sea where they would encounter two mountains. They named their newfound homeland *Ometepec* or *Ometepetl*, two mountains.

Their arrival heralded the beginning of Nicaragua's history, according to the essayist and poet Pablo Antonio Cuadra, who during his long life had constantly been searching for the roots of his homeland. He considered Ometepe to be the "most authentic and expressive symbol" of Nicaragua. Cuadra argues, it is with good reason that the national coat of arms depicts volcanoes rising from the waters. In turn, Ometepe's volcanoes, the one fiery and explosive, the other eternally quiet, embody the essence of the Nicaraguan soul: how it is divided, or split.

Sandino versus Somoza. The paradox of Tiscapa has dogged Nicaragua from its very beginnings. The peaceful Chorotega's were at loggerheads with the warlike Nahuas. With the arrival of the Spaniards, the Indians fell to the sword of the *conquistadores*. Indians and Spaniards, the conquerors and their subjects intermingled: the *mestizo* was born. And ever since independence at the beginning of the nineteenth century the country has been embroiled in one civil war after another. The last one ending in 1990.

According to Cuadra, the one thing people in Nicaragua do not disagree about is the art of poetry. And the only symbol belonging to all Nicaraguans is Rubén Dario, one of the greatest poets in the Spanish language, who was the first to express the – split – nature of Nicaraguan consciousness. "I always wish to be the other," was how Dario put his homeland's duality into words. His line of verse on the 100 *córdoba* banknote reads: "If the homeland is small, you dream it is great." Nicaragua is a country of talkers, one often says, because there is a poet in the soul of every Nicaraguan.

Pablo Antonio Cuadra found signs of duality everywhere. What about the two seasons, summer and winter, the dry and wet times of year? Or the landscape itself? The lakes and volcanoes – in "rough harmony", he wrote after Rubén Dario – form a "hostile merger of the powerful fire of our hills and the serene calmness of our waters".

In light of that, there is not a better place than the island of Ometepe for what I have come to do: to write a book about Nicaragua.

We are nearing the shoreline. In the lee of the island the waves have disappeared. The way Concepción now majestically towers above the calm water, makes you understand how Ometepe got its nickname: Queen of the Lake.

My neighbor has opened his eyes.

"Ometepe has peace and quiet," he says.

He should know, because he was born and raised here. The past few days he had to be in Managua. An awful city. Hot, filthy, noisy, with all that traffic. And the crime. Managua is not a safe place to live.

"Give me the island any day."

The coastline is concealed by tropic vegetation. Thick clusters of green through which pokes the odd crown of a palm tree. The Reina moors at the Moyogalpa pier. The passengers all jostle their way off the ferry.

The main road around Concepción starts in the center of town. Running through the capital city of Altagracia, the road naturally swings back to Moyogalpa. The Magdalena is an hour away. Outside Moyogalpa the paved surface ends and the road turns into a wide, dusty path leading through Esquipulas, Los Angeles, and San José del Sur, where it starts to ascend. After the climb you look out over the wide bay in between the two volcanoes.

The Madera turnoff is a little past Urbaite. From here you drive into the Isthmus of Istián, that connects the volcanoes. Geologists assume that once there used to be two separate islands, which became one as a result of volcanic eruptions. The road runs closely along the long beach of Santo Domingo. Fine grains of white sand are strewn across the surface. Dunes have formed here and there. After the beach, the condition of the road worsens, it leads over cobblestones and is littered with potholes, running up and down, to Balgüe, one of the first villages on the slopes of Madera.

I walk up the slope towards the volcano past wooden huts, the last houses on the village outskirts, through a field of banana and then into the forest. I wonder whether the blocks of stone strewn here and there were once spewed from the mouth of the volcano. Cawing *urracas* take to the sky. The path crosses the dry bed of a brook and leads up, out of the forest. I am now wading through knee high bushes. On the hill in front of me the roof of a small wooden shed with faded, flaking white walls appears. The gate next to it is open. Entering the *finca* I walk along the corral where horses and cows are huddling together. To my left is the main building with the storehouses and the dormer above them, from which there is a breathtaking view of the lake. Faded red letters adorn the front. Two letters are missing, but it is easy to make out the name: MAGDALENA.

I climb up the stone flight of stairs to the porch. Music and smoke are coming out of the kitchen. The floorboards creak. Two parakeets fly past, twittering. Howler monkeys can be heard on the distant forest slopes of the Madera. A breeze rustles through the fronds of a palm tree. Without a sound, a white heron soars down towards the lake, which is turning a lighter shade now the sun is setting behind the Concepción. From steel blue to soft grey. A small cap of cloud is suspended above the volcano again. In a downward direction, the pallid blue of the sky along the western slope transforms into a burning orange stripe above the dark isthmus. Nearby, the short trunk of a *genízaro* stands out, its branches like fingers pointing to the darkening heavens above.

"All of a sudden I wonder why I have to tell this," Julio Cortázar wonders in one of his most beautiful stories. While writing, the writer dwells on the need to write, and then, as a kind of answer, he writes: "but if I begin to ask questions, I'll never tell anything; I'd be better off telling, maybe to tell would be like an answer, at least for someone who is reading it."

THE MAGDALENA

Es que somos muy pobres
The fact is we are very poor
Juan Rulfo

At the crack of dawn the roosters begin to crow and the pigs to grunt. When I leave my room at six in the morning to go downstairs the women are already at work, sitting at the long table. There is a pile of coffee beans on the middle. The women have brought their children. After all, they too can help thresh the beans.

Down another flight of stairs, I reach the kitchen, where I hear the radio playing softly like on every morning. Blanca has already lit the fire. She takes a pot of boiled plantains off the heat and stirs the beans that are simmering next to the rice.

"Aha, Maarten," she replies as usual to my good morning greeting, before turning her daily gaze of contentment out the window. The fire is burning, she is listening to her favorite radio station, Radio Tigre, the day has begun.

I jog down the path through the fields of banana that lead to Balgüe. Farmers coming up the other way on foot or horseback greet me. The villagers too say hello. They have already grown accustomed to the 'gringo' doing his stretching exercises on the village square every morning, before running back up the hill.

At the gate in front of the Magdalena, I stop and catch my breath. Then I make my way across the yard and climb the short flight of stairs to the porch. The men have arrived. They have come to have breakfast before their working day begins. One by one they carry a plastic cup into the kitchen where Blanca serves them. Rice, beans and boiled plantain.

"So," Feliciano hollers, with that ubiquitous smile of his, "how are these fists doing?"

Scarcely having caught my breath I raise a clenched fist and walk up the two flights of stairs to my bedroom. Guests sleep in the old orange storage area, two large rooms at the front of the building. They have given me the room at the back. There is a cabinet, a bed and a writing table. Hanging from a beam on the ceiling is a corn sack filled with sand and sawdust, which they have hung for me a couple of days earlier. I throw open the shutters and look out over the piles of coffee beans, that are drying on the concrete patios below. A large area of pastureland stretches up the slope to where the forest begins, and as on most mornings it vanishes in the clouds that shroud a large part of the Madera.

To the young boys my training is an attraction. As soon as I start jabbing at the corn sack, they jostle each other near the door. Today, Franklin, my most loyal fan, is the only one around. He comes in at seven thirty and goes and sits on the window sill. He hardly ever speaks, but sometimes says the strangest things. "I'm an Indian," he said one time. Or: "I'm sick." Now, as I stand catching my breath, he says: "I'm going to Granada tomorrow and I'm never coming back." His brother lives in Granada and he can box really good. He has already won plenty of bouts.

"And you?" he wants to know.

"I've never boxed a match in my life."

He does not believe me.

"It's true. This will be my first time."

When I am finished and sit there sweating, he grabs my gloves and starts wildly pummeling away at the corn sack. He gives me a daring look. I tell him we ought to train some. Show me a left jab. And a right. One-two. Ok, now a left hook. Left, right, hook and another right. Left, right. He soon loses interest, pulls off the gloves and runs outside.

"Bread, honey, juice and fruit?" Yadira asks when I take my place at the dinner table on the porch.

"And coffee."

"And coffee. Hot coffee, right?"

She laughs, holding a handkerchief in front of her mouth. If you ask me, she and Blanca still cannot believe I would rather not have rice and beans for breakfast. Not even an egg. And does steam really have to come from the coffee?

Yadira brings breakfast. Tomorrow they are going to pull the other front tooth, she says. She is ashamed. That's why she is using the handkerchief.

After breakfast I sit at the edge of the porch to smoke a cigarette. There is a drumming sound. Off to one side cattle and horses come rushing in a cloud of dust, rising together with the dull roar from the drove of animal bodies. Above it all, the shrill cracking of the whip and the 'move 'em up' and 'whoa whoa' of the cowboy can be heard, driving the cattle into the corral. The beasts rush over to the drinking troughs and spread out in all directions when they have had their fill. The long wait has begun. A colt is standing behind a mare, its mother one would assume. Both of them droop their heads and stand equally still. A cow rubs its neck across the trunk of a tree in the middle of the corral. A horse scratches its hindquarters against the gate. A brief and violent squall of rain lashes down, which leaves the animals unperturbed. The horses all stand with their long necks hanging in the same direction. A heroic aura of submission emanates from the animal still life I am observing. The world could end but still you would not be able to see little more than the slightest twitch of a mane or shiver down the back. Waiting, and nothing else, until the cowboy takes them back out to pasture again.

I go back to my room and sit down at the writing table. Outside, I see the sow crossing over the patio. Juan comes running and chases it away. "One big latrine, that patio of ours," he once said to me. But now, with all those coffee beans, lying there to dry …

Two farmers are making their way up the mountain path. I watch them until they have disappeared behind the trees. The cloudbank is already showing signs of breaking up and the green of the volcano appears. I sometimes feel the same way about the stories that I am writing at this table: snatches of a tropical sky that constantly looks different, the clouds move, open and close, vanish and re-appear, concealing and then again revealing the green mystery that lies behind them.

In front of me are the notes of my conversations with Evert Lezama, an agronomist I got to know when he spent a couple of months at Magdalena to offer organizational advice to the cooperative.

He told me about his hometown of León, purportedly the first town to be liberated in Nicaragua. The *guerilleros* of the *Frente Sandinista* fought Somoza's army from the mountains. Evert always thought: "I want to be like those people," and even though he was much too young, he still joined the struggle. Because of his cousin Cristóbal, who had been in the resistance for years. They were inseparable. Cristóbal was his example, a kind of older brother. Once Evert came into his room and saw a weapon there. Made in Israel and captured from the National Guard. Then Cristóbal told him all kinds of things. About the arms the *Frente* and National Guard each used. Later, in the army, Evert found out for himself how you can hear the difference. The FAL, the standard issue rifle of the contras, made a dull thudding sound, while the Sandinista AKs sounded at a much higher pitch. Cristóbal also told him about the situation in the country, that Somoza was a dictator, that the farmers did not own any land, but that everything was in the hands of one man. This marked the beginning of Evert's political awareness, you knew why you were fighting: for a just society and land that was evenly distributed.

Normally speaking, you had to pass a test, by placing a bomb for instance, or by luring the Guards into an ambush, or robbing a bank to get money for the Revolution. But at the time, Evert was thirteen and much too young. In the beginning, he rode around town on his bicycle keeping an eye on what the Guards were doing.

When the guerrillas had come down out of the mountains in 1978 and headed towards the city, things had become grimmer and more harsh. If the army caught you, you could forget it. You would be grilled in the Fortín, the most hated place of the National Guard, its headquarters, arms depot and place of torture. Or you just disappeared and were found dead days later along the side of the road along the outskirts.

Evert explained that the Fortín was situated at a higher elevation overlooking the city. When they began bombarding the city from there, a battle broke out that raged for three days until Liberation Day. Evert fought in the rear guard, but he was there on the seventh, when the National Guard were driven back and fled. In fact, everyone was there. If you were not fighting, you brought food or tended to the wounded. The people had liberated themselves. On July 7th in León.

After that the dirty war had began. With the Sandinsta army Evert joined in attacks on National Guard troops, or *contras* as they were now called. They fought in the mountains in the north of the country, from Wiwilí right into Honduras, where the contras were being trained and armed by the Americans. Evert told me the local population suffered most from the fighting. If they knew where the contras were hiding they fired rockets at them and when you entered a village afterwards you came across the charred remains of body parts, arms, legs, beaten against trees or strewn over the ground. Often the only way for the people to save themselves was to go with the contras. Of course they were just as bad, they had leveled as many villages themselves. You saw corpses hanging from tree branches, arms and legs bound, testicles cut off and stuffed into mouths, bodies ripped open, their intestines dangling in the wind. Vultures circling overhead.

You were in constant fear, Evert told me. War was: keeping your wits about you, two minutes here, two minutes there, looking, to the left, to the right, in front, behind, staying alert, always on your guard, never too long in any one spot, but also never moving without good reason. Always fear. And longing to go back home to your family. Evert told himself that if he did not make any mistakes, he would survive.

"You don't want to die, it's just instinct," he said.

The questions had started coming after the war. You had fought against the contras because they were undermining the revolution, but in actual fact the United States had imposed the war because they did not want a second Cuba. That is why all those boys had to die. Boys scarcely familiar with the sound of rifle shots and the smell of gun powder and then *ratatatat*, bam, boom, bang, running for it and turning into easy targets. And what good had their deaths done? What it had amounted to was that they were supposed to wipe out the contras and the contras them, that fellow countrymen were battling it out with one another.

Evert had taken part in six major battles. That was the only time he was not afraid, when the shooting began, then fear changed into rage, you felt it rising from the pit of your stomach and you felt strength and euphoria because you and your seventy comrades were going to shoot the hell out of those bastards.

What followed was loneliness. Victims lay strewn all around you, but you had to go on. Alone, because on the frontline, you could not make any friends. If they were killed, you would never be able to carry on. That is why, for weeks on end, you found yourself with boys you did not want to get to know, in the mountains where nobody wanted to be. You were hungry, it was cold, everyone was scared and everybody thought of home, while your AK was the only mother or father who could save your life.

Fear, Evert told me, has many faces. He was scared while standing guard at night. Staring into the darkness and listening to the sounds of the forest, really made him feel the loneliness and all he thought about was leaving.

When he finally did come back from the front, he still supported the Revolution, because it benefited the people, but without the conviction of the time before his military service, while teaching people to read and write, or during the work for the Revolution, the red and black labor, picking cotton and coffee. Because things were not like they had initially promised. It had become totalitarian and militaristic. There were more arms in Nicaragua than people. Everything they said was law, the newspaper *La Prensa* was banned and the official press only reported Sandinista army victories. The dead did not exist. "I don't want to be a part of this puppet show anymore," Evert had told the Sandinistas. He was lucky not to have been picked up, because before you knew it you would have the State Security Service breaking down your neck. You were one of us, or one of them.

The thing that appalled him most about the party to mark the end of the 1990 Frente election campaign was that they thought it was a foregone conclusion they would win. Red and black headbands were all over the place, a bottle of rum in every hand, protest songs being sung just like old times. They were flushed with victory even before the elections had taken place. But the people decided otherwise. The people had not let themselves be taken for a ride. There was rationing going on, people waited for hours for a couple of eggs or a piece of bread, and then there was that loathsome compulsory military service. A great many mothers had voted against. And after the elections, the *piñata* saw to it they lost the last vestiges of support from those who still believed in them.

Once democracy took over, Evert said, every Nicaraguan had a say in how he thought the country ought to be run. That is what peace had achieved. But the ideals had been betrayed, he thought, the parties were only out for their share of power.

"Nicaragua has always been treated like a whore," he said. "Our laws are there to be broken."

The new leaders were working for their own friends, the wealthy who had fled to Miami when the Revolution began and who wanted their properties back. And the Sandinistas were still shouting about the struggle. The struggle for land, the struggle for peace, for brotherhood, for solidarity, the struggle for the preservation of rule of law, you name it.

"But confrontations lead nowhere," said Evert. "The people don't want any more bloodshed. Another war and we won't even be able to afford a pair of pants, let alone underpants, nothing."

I get up from behind my writing table and walk to the front of the building, to the dormer with the panoramic view of the lake, where Evert and I had sat talking. It is after twelve, time for the midday meal. The farmers are already back from the land. They have been busy picking coffee during November and December. Now in January, there is less work. After the usual bowl of rice and beans with boiled plantain, most of them head for home. Let the women do the threshing. Juan stays put, which makes sense because he and Blanca live at Magdalena while she is running the kitchen. Feliciano does not live there, but he too stays a little longer almost every day. As chairman of the cooperative there is always something for him to do. Bernabé is still around too. He is in the warehouse, where the coffee is stored when the women are finished threshing the beans. The bales of orange plastic are piled higher and higher. It has been a good year, says Bernabé as he walks outside. The harvest is twice what it was last year. Behind the door with which he closes the warehouse, a mural of Sandino emerges, even though it is not easy to recognize the freedom fighter in it. There is so little left of his portrait, Bernabé puts forward, because it dates from the time the cooperation had just began operations in the early eighties.

Tired and filthy, the archaeologists trickle in. One heads straight for the shower, another flops down on a couch and looks at the sketches made during the day. Yadira sets the table. Soon all twenty of them are having their meal. They are on a six week stay at the farmstead. This is the fourth time their team leader Susan has been here. In the vicinity of Magdalena alone, they have charted more than two thousand petroglyphs, along with earthenware, shrines and cemeteries. And yet Ometepe remains a mystery. The general assumption is that the rock engravings date from 800 A.D. They contain depictions of animals and humans. But what do all these circles and spirals signify?

The story goes that a young Nicaraguan researcher had his hands on the solution to the enigma. He purportedly met an old man, who had asked him whether he, as a researcher, might happen to know the secret of the circles and spirals. The young man had said he did not, whereupon the old man flew into a rage and shouted at the poor researcher: "Then you don't know anything at all!" And he went on to reveal to him the mysteries behind Ometepe's circles and spirals. Stunned as he was, the researcher had forgotten to take notes and asked the old man to tell him the story again, but he had cloaked himself in silence, saying only "the sacred must be kept in the deepest recesses of the soul."

The sound of whistling can be heard from the corral. I turn around and see the cowboy and three young lads driving the cattle out to pasture. The corral is left behind, big and empty. At the edge of the water troughs are four white herons with their heads sagging deep between their shoulders. They don't even look up, not even at the whinnying of the one horse the cowboy has left behind, tugging at the rope that hitches him.

It does not take long before the cowboy and the three lads return. They have three calves with them, which they put under a lean-to beside the corral. After the cowboy has dug his spurs into his horse and ridden off, the lads lead one of the calves into the corral and let it loose. The biggest boy throws a lasso around the animal's throat, jumps on its back and tries to ride it. Terrified, the calf bucks up and down from his front to hind legs. Then a smaller boy dares to climb on the back of the calf. He scarcely manages to hang on and falls to the ground after being bucked around a few times to the loud laughter and cheering of his buddies.

Boleros from the kitchen – cries lamenting the immense pain of love – are the soundtrack to the setting sun. There is an orange glow on the slopes of the Concepción. The grunting of a pig passing by accompanies the music, as does the crowing of the black rooster with its bright red comb and wattles, chasing after a chicken. It seems as if all that sound is washing over the scenery, across the porch and down towards the lake and then, in the distance, up the slopes of the Concepción.

Even the setting sun seems to be rolling to the steady beat coming from the kitchen. *El amor es una trampa, una trampa maldita.* (Love is a trap, a wicked trap). No one can pull a fast one on Blanca, leaning there in the open window next to her radio. Master of all she surveys, she watches another day gently swaying to its end. The look of satisfaction on her smiling face betrays a rock-solid certainty: life is good, as long as there is Radio Tigre.

THE MATCH

For José Angel *Vampiro* Meléndez Córdoba

Oscar *Burro* Alemán is smoking a cigarette at the entrance. He takes a drag and lazily raises his eyes.

"Back again?"

Alemán looks at his stopwatch and shuffles inside ahead of me. The gym is under the stands of the stadium in Managua. Light falls on the bare slab of concrete floor through two barred windows in the wall. Four concrete pillars bear the ceiling that gradually tapers. At the back four punching bags hang in a row.

"Time!" Alemán calls.

His boys, in the left corner, take a breather and wait for him to come with the water bottle. Last year I had quickly got tired of *Burro* and changed to the other corner within a few weeks. A black boy is going at the bag there.

"Come on, left, right!" *Vampiro* shouts at him from the middle of the gym. "One-two! and left hook! Do you call those punches? You have to be sharp. Hit quicker! And harder! Look."

Vampiro shows him a dazzling combination.

"Keep your defense up. Hands high. And now four jabs. Left, right, hook, right, come on, sharper!"

He turns away with a sigh and walks towards the pillar to his water bottle. He checks his watch and signals to his pupils.

"That's enough. Come here."

The boys gather round him. Vampiro pours water down their throats. He puts the bottle on the floor and strolls away, humming a tune: "…pa, pa, pa."

I tap him on the shoulder from behind. He slowly turns around and sizes me up from top to bottom. A cautious smile spreads across his face.

"Gringo!"

"Gringo?"

"Ah, German!"

"German?"

"Oh yeah, Dutchman!"

"Dutchman, yeah."

"Dutch, damn! Are you gonna start training again?"

"And fighting."

He claps his hands.

"Now you're talking! I'll get you ready in a month."

I scowl. We walk over to the corner where there's a beat up old desk with his gear on it. Vampiro leans against the desk and shouts "ok, let's get cracking again!" to his boys. He lights a cigarette and looks at me with a glint of interrogation in his eye.

"I was thinking more like May," I say.

Vampiro grumbles in protest. It's January now. So let's go for March, won't three months be more than enough? But for the time being I'm going to be in Ometepe, I tell him. I'll only be in Managua once a week, at most. Vampiro growls at me with a mischievous grin.

"Not with *Burro* this time?"

"What for? I can keep my eye on the clock and carry my own water."

"A ha," he crows. "So, you finally figured it out. Panama's the place to be, if you wanna box. We've got salsa! Those Nicaraguans are no good. I tell them straight to their face. All talk, but good for nothing."

At the end of my first stay in Nicaragua, seven months ago now, a man who looked like a used car salesman had walked into the gym. He had inquired about my weight and said he could arrange a fight. I had told him that I was not interested in fighting matches. He insisted and I had reacted he should get in touch when the time was ripe. Honestly speaking, it had never occurred to me to go and fight an actual match. I was just training. But the thought had a romantic appeal. The ring, the corner, the bell, a knock-out. Somewhere at the back of my mind, I was intrigued. Vampiro was all for it. You box to fight. But the man never came back.

I considered including a story about boxing in my book about Nicaragua. Boxing, along with baseball, is Nicaragua's most important sport. Suddenly, the romantic notion was within reach: the best thing would be if I were to play the lead role in the story myself.

Bouts are held practically every week in Managua. The scene of the action is the *Gimnasio Alexis Argüello,* or *Alexis*, as it is simply called, named after Nicaragua's greatest boxer of all time. Argüello won his first of many world champion belts in 1974 by defeating the Mexican boxing legend Rubén Olivares. In international boxing circles, he is still remembered for his legendary technique.

"Alexis is the best thing Nicaragua has ever produced," says Vampiro without equivocation, "one of Latin America's all-time greatest boxers."

Vampiro should know: he was Argüellos' sparring partner in the mid nineteen seventies. His own career was drawing to a close, after nearly twenty years. Vampiro had got started young. At the age of fifteen, a month and a half after putting on gloves, he was already in the ring. Two years on he fought his first professional bout. He had to. His mother had died, and he blamed his father.

"I said: 'Listen up, old man, you're the way you are, and I'm the way I am, and we just don't get along.'"

Vampiro left home and had to make money. He succeeded. His arms outstretched to the sky, he says:

"God helped me get there."

In total he fought seventy-nine bouts, sixteen as an amateur, winning fifty-two, losing twenty-three and with four undecided matches. He fought in Colombia, Venezuela, Ecuador, Peru, Brazil and Argentina. Vampiro was champion of Panama at the age of twenty-three.

"I left there, because my girlfriend cheated on me. I loved her, so I thought: 'I'm out of here.'"

He first went to Costa Rica, where he fought and won two fights. Then Nicaragua, seven wins. Then further to the north. El Salvador, Guatemala, Mexico.

"I've always boxed. I love money, so you have to. Even fought in New York. Brooklyn, all black dudes there. One knock-out, one defeat."

He headed back to Panama in a Volvo. With five hundred dollars in his pocket and a check for ten thousand dollars in his suitcase.

"I never made it past Nicaragua."

He is not half bad as a trainer, if he says so himself. In three years time he has coached two national and one Central American champion. In the juvenile division. No, the big money still awaits. For the time being he has to make sure he gets his fifty *córdobas* a month per pupil, or at least thirty if they cannot afford it. But hey, it is not easy for them either.

"When I see those kids on the street, with hardly any clothes, begging, shining shoes, washing windshields. It's a crying shame. I always tell my boys here to be careful. That they shouldn't steal, drink liquor, do drugs. But then there are always those who are just weaklings. Check it out, that kid there, hey black man, keep punching! Tall, fast, strong, you can see, but he won't make it. He's a pansy. Two fights, two losses. I could tell right away the second time, this guy is going down, so I threw the towel into the ring. You're not going to let them get the shit beaten out of them, are you?"

Vampiro stops talking and lights another cigarette. After a deep drag he says with great conviction: "Some day I'm going to make a champion out of one of these boys. So help me God."

He looks down at his watch and shouts: "Ok guys, one more minute. Let's mix it up. Come on!"

He looks at me again.

"Phew, what a bunch of sissies. What am I supposed to do with these guys?"

He laughs and claps his hands.

"Dutchman! Damn!"

A few weeks later I'm in town for a couple of days and go over to the gym to train. Vampiro feints around me in circles during a bout of shadow boxing.

"Use your length, German. Keep your distance, and tease. Left, left, left. And step in when you can, jab, bam, bam, bam, and get out, 'cos you gotta get out of that hell. Show me that left hand, Dutchman. Wallop that guy."

Nicaraguans are all a bunch of pansies, he says, I'll find out soon enough. You got to hit them and then hit them again, that scares them.

"Faster, quicker!" he shouts at Rodrigo who is working on the bag, "and keep moving."

"Move, gringo," he shouts at me. "Boxing is salsa. Dancing. It's all in the hips."

Rodrigo is about to fight his first professional bout, says Vampiro as I stand catching my breath after my round, and it's about time, since he has already had more than fifty fights. He has a contract for one thousand *córdobas*, win or lose. Not bad by a long shot, for a first bout, thinks Vampiro.

"And what did you make in your day?"

"Dollars."

"How much?"

"Three hundred, five hundred, eight hundred. A match. Hey, back in the seventies, a beer didn't even cost a dime."

"The good life, eh?"

"What do you think?"

He sticks his thumbs under imaginary suspenders.

"Vampiro Meléndez! Ha! Nice clothes, friends, women. A class act! No, I had nothing to complain about."

We walk back to his desk. There is more to it than just dancing, says Vampiro. It's also about skill, the little wrinkles and the secrets. Looking, for instance. In Panama, the first thing you learn is to look at your opponent's footwork, so you know what he is going to do next. If he steps to the left, a left handed punch will follow. To the right, a right. Later on, you learn to look him in the eye. Whatever he does, you keep looking at him, because there are always some frigging pansies who can't take it. Look, move, jab, turn. All at once. In Panama they call it *boxear*."

Vampiro sits down on the desk and tells me about his heyday, back in the seventies. Under Somoza anything went. Besides, in those days he was into everything. Those trips during Easter to the beach. Money in your pocket and whatever you wanted!

"Why did you take up with the guerrillas then, for heaven's sake?"

"Because those guys in the *Guardia* went too far. You saw so many people being oppressed."

In 1978 Vampiro joined the *Frente* movement. He puffs out his chest and smacks his right hand on his left shoulder: "Colonel Vampiro."

He took part in operations from out of Costa Rica and celebrated victory with the Sandinistas in Managua in July 1979, when the revolution was a fact. Afterwards he fought in the army, until his leg was crippled from the impact of a mortar round. He knows practically all the commanders personally; he fought with them side by side. Not a year earlier, Tomás Borge called him on the phone, Tomasito, one of the *Frente* founding fathers. Sixty-six years old. Did Vampiro want to teach him how to box? He scratches under his black FSLN baseball cap.

"I became a Nicaraguan for those guys."

He was crazy about the country when he came here for the first time. God knows why.

"Nowadays, you really ask yourself, when you see what a mess it has become, whether it was all worth it. But," he says fiercely while getting to his feet, "people shouldn't tell me any of their cock and bull stories. I am a Sandinista until the day I die!"

He is never going back to Panama. His life is here. When he left the army they gave him a plot of land. That's where his house is. He has a wife and a son. Vampiro lifts up his baseball cap and smiles bashfully. He is going bald and his hair is graying at the temples.

"Besides, I'm already past fifty."

From his desk he walks back into the arena and starts humming.

"*Tanto tiempo…pa, pa, pa.*"

PACIFICO

DOCTOR RAMÍREZ

The inner courtyard of the *Casa de los Leones* exudes the dignified repose of colonial Nicaragua, a land of silent patios and umbrageous arcades. A cleaning lady slowly and quietly swishes her mop across the tile floor of the gallery. Coming from a room is the rattling sound of a typewriter. I am late for my appointment with *doctor* Ramírez, director of the municipal archives. Impatiently, I follow the doorman shuffling in front of me. On the other side of the patio he shows me to a tiny office. A respectable looking man, his straight hair parted impeccably down the middle, wearing an ironed pin-striped shirt, looks up phlegmatically.

"Doctor Ramírez?"

He nods and says:

"You're late."

I offer my apologies, to which Ramírez replies that it is almost time for him to leave. He asks whether we might reschedule our talk for tomorrow. He would however be happy to show me the archives. It proves to be the office cabinet behind his desk. Most of the documents were lost through storms, rain, plundering and theft, Ramírez remarks.

"We received this cabinet from the British embassy," he says. "We have no funding, you see."

Ramírez has an apologetic glint in his eyes.

"I work here at no personal benefit to myself."

He straightens up a bit in his chair.

"The British will see that serious work is being conducted here. In this country one is apt, how shall I put it, to be a bit slipshod when it comes to foreign aid, wouldn't you say, our pockets are rather deep."

We both share a smile and reschedule our appointment for the next day.

From the Mombacho volcano, that rises to the west of Granada, the only thing you can make out are the two white towers of the city's cathedral and the crowns of the palm trees on the square in front of it. Granada lies like a tiny dot on the shores of the endless lake. *Mar Dulce*, the Sweet Sea, as the Spaniards used to call Lake Nicaragua, is one hundred and eighty kilometers long and sixty kilometers wide. It has sawfish and the only species of freshwater shark in the world. Shipping is negligible. A few fishing boats or a ferry on its way to Ometepe or the mouth of the San Juan river at the other end.

In history books the lake is considered both a blessing and a curse to Granada. Early on in the sixteenth century the Spanish discovered that the San Juan river provided a navigable route to the Caribbean Sea, behind which lay the Atlantic and hence their homeland. Commodities came to Granada from every corner of Central America to be shipped to Spain. No other city in the region was as prosperous. But wealth also attracted pirates. Granada was plundered and reduced to ashes by buccaneers several times.

Perhaps the pirates used the archipelago just to the south of the city as their safe haven. Today small boats are moored there for trips along the more than three hundred volcanic islets, some of which are no bigger than a small house with a modest yard. The dirt road leading to Granada runs through the tourist center from the Sandinista era. One long strip of restaurants, dance clubs, boarding houses and picnic areas, along the beach of the big lake where it is always windy and the waves are always high. Further on, there where the broad boulevard begins towards the city center, is the bronze statue of Francisco Hernández de Córdoba, the conquistador, who founded Granada in 1524, and later on that same year the city of León, Nicaragua's other major city from the colonial era.

The houses along the boulevard look bright and cheerful with their gables of pastel yellow, bright blue or soft red. People are lazing in rocking chairs in front of their homes. "Those not forced by hunger to work, lie in a hammock all day long or sit in front of an open window under an azure tropical sky, in perfect enjoyment of the complete state of inertia that people regard as life", wrote a disgruntled German scientist a century ago.

The boulevard ends at Granada's central square. The fronds of the tall palm trees glisten in the bright rays of sun, that reflect from the towers of the cathedral in blinding white light. The fountain in the middle of the square is dry. Judging by the weeds in the basin, it has been quite a while since any water has come out the mouths of the angels and nymphs. In front of the elegant Alhambra hotel a number of coachman are hanging around their horse and buggies. There are no clients for a guided tour.

I walk up the steps of the *Club Social* next door. I should go and have a look, now that it was still possible, Ramírez had told me. The yellow ochre of its austere front has just been repainted. The mosaic floor of the reception hall has recently been re-laid along with the mirrored tiles of the ballroom. Gnashing their teeth, the Granadian elite had witnessed how the Sandinistas had annexed their exquisite social club to transform it into a revolutionary cultural center. But now the rich are demanding their club back. The chandelier hanging from the white stucco ceiling is ready for use, except for a few missing light bulbs. It will not be long before the holiest of the holy will once again belong to the *happy few*. Admittance only for members and their guests.

The cathedral clocks begin to chime at six o'clock. The enormous doors swing open. People have come in droves to witness the arrival of Maria, who is now being taken through the streets on a cart. Every day in the first week of December the Virgin crosses through a district in Granada. She receives the cheers of the people living in the neighborhood, weeping for her on the sidewalks, pleading with her to answer their prayers and following her to the cathedral.

There she is. In front of the church gates she is lifted from the cart. Above the applause and cheering of the multitude, that now fills the entire square, fireworks erupt in an earsplitting din. The Virgin passes by the pews packed with people and is set down on the altar. The faithful start to throng around her, shedding tears, murmuring prayers and repeating their wishes. An unbroken line of people shuffle past until late in the evening. There is a constant barrage of fireworks outside. Young people are having a good time on the square. There is dancing, laughter and, behind the bushes, kissing.

The next day, doctor Ramírez warns that the daytime serenity and exuberant night life are not what they seem. Behind Granada's cheerful looking facades hides the iron hand of the elite: the *criollos* who took over from the Spaniards after independence in 1821. Ramírez starts by telling about the colonial era, when the governors of Nicaragua resided in the *Casa de los Leones*. The finest theater companies in Europe came to perform here. This building was destroyed halfway through the nineteenth century at the hands of the dreaded American sea pirate William Walker.

Ramírez has laid an 1869 edition of a book on the table. It contains the deed of transfer of William Walker's sword. A gift from the government of Honduras, where he was shot before a firing squad, Ramírez explains.

"The sword," are the opening words to the flowery sentence, on which he has laid his finger, "is bestowed upon Granada as an immortal trophy against the tyrant of Nicaragua."

Supported by a mercenary army of barely a hundred men, Walker had been able to outwit a weakened Nicaragua in the throes of rivalry between Granada and León, and have himself declared president of the republic. It took two years before the combined armies of Nicaragua, Costa Rica and Honduras could defeat the occupier, but not before he and his cronies had plundered and reduced Granada to little more than a smoking pile of ruins.

"All that remained of the Casa de los Leones, was the gateway," says Ramírez.

The departure of the scourge heralded a period of great growth, he continues. Trade flourished. Granada enhanced its townscape with handsome buildings in neo-classical style, and finally came out of the shadow of León. After independence, the two rival cities had been continually out for one another's blood and had dragged Nicaragua into one civil war after the other. But León could not compete with Granada's commercial power. It lost its rights as capital city, during the administration of President Fruto Chamorro from Granada. The Chamorro family made their fortune at the end of the nineteenth century. Ever since, together with the Sacasa, Cuadra and Pellas families, the Chamorros make up the core of Granadian high society, the 'aristocracy', as Ramírez mockingly refers to them.

"And the sword?" I ask.

"Vanished. No one knows where it is, but rumor has it that mayor Alejandro Chamarro gave it to the Sacasa family in the early twentieth century."

Ramírez shrugs his shoulders.

"That's the way it goes. That sword probably adorns a mantelpiece in someone's chic living room. It will no doubt surface someday."

He turns his attention back to the book.

"Look here, this document was written by one of my ancestor's, a Marenco, who has been mayor of Granada. At the moment the Marenco family has a representative in parliament. They too belong to the aristocracy." Ramírez looks me in the eye. "But not from our side of the family."

Over the years the aristocrats have been able to maintain their economic power, he tells me. They tolerated Somoza as long as he left them in peace and worked for his downfall when he had gone too far during his last years. Politically speaking, the elite have little influence.

"They would have to build a bridge to the people, but they turn their noses up at that."

I give him a business card when saying goodbye. He looks at it attentively and puts it into his breast pocket.

"Thanks. I gave you mine yesterday, didn't I?"

I hesitate, cannot remember anything about it. It must be my failing memory.

"Yes," I say without much conviction.

The guests trickle into the reception area of the Saint Francis monastery. Women decked out in old-fashioned, but elegant evening dresses and in a cloud of the latest scents from Paris are welcomed by personnel clad in black and white. Their husbands panting in their wake, squeezed into three piece suits combined with wide ties drawn tight, are wiping the perspiration from their faces gone red with exertion. It is six o'clock in the evening and hot.

A sigh of disappointment shudders through the crowd when the vice-president is announced instead of the president. Nevertheless, her words more than fit the occasion, judging by the look on everyone's faces. Mrs. Julia Mena, who reminds those present that she too is a born Granadian, impresses upon her audience that today's reopening of the city's oldest monastery after a lengthy period of restoration does indeed live up to Granada's name. She praises the courage of her fellow citizens, who have overcome the blows of fate time and time again and commends the Catholic disposition of her listeners. Then she calls to mind the legend of the virgin of Granada. After all, it is the beginning of December.

Once upon a time, she says, a long long time ago, a group of native women were washing their clothes on the shores of the lake. One of them noticed something floating in the waves. It came closer and they saw it was a small chest, but every time the women thought they would be able to grab it, it floated away again. Priests passing by came to lend them a hand and were able to drag the little chest onto the beach. When they had opened the lid, a miracle had taken place. There was a statue of Mary in the chest. No one knew where it had come from, no one knew to whom it belonged. But from that day onward, Granada had its virgin, Mary Immaculate Conception.

"We are a people of Mary's, motherly and conciliatory," Mrs. Mena concludes.

Amid enthusiastic applause she goes ahead of the buzzing crowd to the monastery chapel. Once, Bartolomé de las Casas had delivered thundering sermons here against the maltreatment of the native population by the Spanish conquistadors. Now the guests allow themselves to be intoxicated by the musical strains of the Christmas concert, performed by National Choir of Nicaragua accompanied by the National Orchestra of Nicaragua. No one appears bothered by the false notes hit by the solo vocalists, nor by the poor acoustics of the chapel. In any case, it has not put a damper on the mood afterwards. Elated and contented the guests converse over a block of Dutch cheese and a glass of French white wine. *Doctor* Mena, a gentleman getting on in years in a crumpled pin-striped suit, amiably receives the reverent praise being bestowed upon him. He is, as a journalist tells me, an authority on the history of the city. Mena declares nothing would give him greater satisfaction than to receive me tomorrow at his home, "to clarify any ambiguities."

"Not yet, not yet," says *doctor* Mena the next day wagging his finger at me when we run into each other on the square. His shirt and trousers are bulging at the seams under pressure of his protruding paunch. "And remember: one o'clock sharp. I am a stickler for German punctuality."

I ring the Mena's doorbell exactly on the stroke of one. The *doctor* is not at home, a servant informs me in the doorway. She goes inside to enquire whether it is permitted to let me inside and wait. Yes, it's permitted. The servant shows me to a bench in the hallway. Mena comes in half an hour later and after a lunch of an additional half hour, he invites me with utmost courtesy to take a seat in the corner of the patio. The southeastern corner, where it is coolest at this time of day, he elucidates.

Mena tells me he has traveled extensively. The Netherlands has reclaimed land from the sea, hasn't it? As his tales fan out across all corners of the globe, his eyes slowly begin to close.

"Are you tired?" I ask him when he wakes with a start after having nodded off for a moment.

"No, no, *señor*. Please proceed. It's Granada you want to know more about, isn't it? Ask anything you want. You see, my ancestors go all the way back to the conquistadores. I can tell you everything."

Mena holds forth about the blessings bequeathed to these parts owing to the Spanish intervention. Only the undaunted and steadfast disposition of the Spaniard could be deemed capable of enlightening this barbaric darkness with his intrinsic civilization and especially with the one and only True word, for shouldn't the grand design of the Spanish Kings first and foremost be considered the fulfillment of a divine mission? Who else but they, the *criollos*, could lay claim, with all due modesty, it goes without saying, to the legacy of age old Spanish traditions, long since enriched with the most refined customs of the highest European caliber? Who else should be bestowed with the leadership of this country, other than those in whose veins course the unadulterated blood of the glorious Spaniard? The *mestizo*, that half-breed, or, worse still, the Indian, totally devoid of culture or civilization? When Mena's eyes again close, I let mine stray along the walls where history remains visible in the portraits of the men I take to be his forefathers. A portrait of the founding forefather will probably not be there. Few conquistadores have spread as much death and destruction in the name of the Spanish Crown as has Pedrarias de Avila. The interference of the conqueror of Nicaragua made God's word sound like the scything of the sword and the lash of the whip. His lust for gold set an example for many an adventurer, though his zeal to spread the true faith among the savages is subject to reasonable doubt. It is said that Pedrarias had disobedient Indians drawn and quartered or fed to his dogs. Nevertheless, he sold most of them to Francisco Pizarro to serve in his campaign of conquest in Peru, where death awaited the Indian on the icy slopes of the Andes.

Pedraria's widow doña Isabel de Bobadilla y Peñaloza was of a more humane persuasion. Genocide would lead to an early demise of Nicaragua, according to doña Isabel, who reversed her husband's logic upon his death: the true gold of the New World did not lie in selling off its people, but precisely in the bellies of its native women. A large *mestizo* population, eternally inferior and subservient to strict Spanish rule, would ensure Spain a cheap army of labor to exploit Nicaragua's inexhaustible riches. And so coupling her humanity with shrewd business sense - since those unfortunate souls doing the dirty work in this barbarous place so far from their beloved fatherland, were entitled to substantial compensation - doña Isabel commissioned the building of a legendary brothel, earning her place in history as the first Madame of the New World. In exchange for golden ducats, the Spanish rank and file could impregnate the fairest Indian daughters, from whose bleeding bellies the eternally tormented *mestizo* first saw the light of day.

This is the story written by the historian Ricardo Pasos in his novel *The Pedrarias Brothel*. The author employs raunchy eroticism to strip the heroic epic of the conquest bare and disclose the traumatic birth of the colony in all its fleshy drama.

Doctor Mena wakes up with a fright. "Where were we? Go ahead, ask me anything. You see, our families ensure a high standard of public morals is maintained. We safeguard the true Catholic faith."

With disgust Mena tells me about the Sandinista era. He should know, since he stayed behind in Granada while most of his fellow aristocrats had gone into exile in Miami.

"Public order had vanished. A farmer has to work his land, like he is supposed to, but at the time nobody worked and everybody came demanding their rights. It is good that these communists are gone."

Now all those families who had left are returning to Nicaragua. Most of them prefer to live in Managua. Mena starts delivering a lamentation about this repulsive city, the chaos, the stench, the crime rate, and what a dreadful climate. When his eyes again begin to shut, I get to my feet and quietly leave the house.

From a distance *doctor* Ramírez is walking towards me, staggering, shirt tails hanging out of his trousers and his hair disheveled.

"Had a little look around town?" he asks with a defiant look in his eyes.

Sluggishly, he brushes a lock of hair from his forehead.

"Well," he continues, "I myself have enjoyed quite an *ethylic* midday meal."

The meaning of his poetic turn of phrase is made abundantly clear by a strong reek of alcohol. Ramírez stares dreamily into space. We are standing on a busy street corner, where the wind and the sound of traffic make it difficult to understand one another.

"You are in another world around here. This is the city center, there's nothing wrong, but there are neighborhoods where you shouldn't go, especially after dark. You'd get stabbed for a couple of pennies."

Ramírez waves his arm in a wide arc.

"This is Nicaragua, a country, how do they put it again, on its way to development. We are not in Europe here, there is no schooling, no development, no culture."

He barely manages to keep from belching.

"My ancestors came from Spain and Italy. But I'm Nicaraguan. And a *criollo*, at that.

Ramírez' laugh is hollow.

"My father lost quite a lot. *Criollo* in name, but without any capital. Hit the skids, you see."

He shrugs his shoulders. "I have been to Miami for four years."

Ramírez bemoans how superficial Americans are.

"To the Yankees, we are all Latinos, just a bunch of scum, all of us crooks."

His fingers grope through an empty pack of cigarettes. I offer him a cigarette, which he accepts and lights.

"It's all about having principles," he resumes after a deep drag. "Which is something the people don't have."

He turns his pants pockets inside out.

"You see. I'm flat broke. I walked ten kilometers to get here, don't even have cab fare."

He gives me a bleary eyed look. There is something beseeching about the grin on his face.

"But I speak English too, you know."

Ramírez pauses and then resumes.

"The past few days I have been helping you with things that have taken me months to dig out of the archive. Other people might ask you for money. Not me, don't worry, my motives have been totally unselfish."

"How about a beer maybe?"

"You do understand what I mean, don't you. It's about principles."

"Of course. My motive for offering you a beer is also fully unselfish."

We enter the first bar we come to. Ramírez tries arrange his hair, but the locks are stubborn and fall back over his forehead.

"Have you already visited the *Club Social*?"

"Yesterday."

"Did you know that in his day, Somoza was never allowed in? An ordinary military man like him, not on your life."

Ramírez was a young man at the time. The *sixties* had not passed by Granada unnoticed. The Beatles, Jimi Hendrix, The Doors, Janis Joplin, the Stones. Lots of marihuana. There was always a party going on somewhere. However, back then, he had other things on his mind. The family maid fell pregnant when he was twenty-two. He was the father. He wanted to keep the baby, so they had a son. He must be in his twenties now.

"They weren't allowed to stay on," he says. "My family, what do you think?"

He slurps on his bottle, his eyes glisten.

41

"One of those foxy black girls from the coast, you understand. Not throwing her out on the street right then and there was something they could not accept."

Ramírez, bent forward in a pensive mood, arches his back and tries to focus. After a stiff swig he scoffs: "Somoza figured he could find good marriage partners for his children at the *Club Social.* Outrageous. Our aristocracy is arrogant and closed. In Granada they only marry each other. The bloodlines and capital have to be kept together. I lost all my friends."

He finishes off his bottle, nods to the bartender for another one and sits there for quite a while, lost in thought.

"I never finished university. It wasn't important back then."

He steals a glance at me.

"Doctor Ramírez does not exist. I am just Carlos Alberto Ramírez and everything I know is my own doing."

"The business card?"

Ramírez nods.

THE CHILDREN OF ADIACT

The cobblestone road leads from Leon's city square past colonial merchant's houses out of the town center. In passing I peek through the barred windows of the Rubén Dario museum. Professor Buitrago is not there. It's still too early, I guess.

A kilometer further on, the straight road runs into an elevated platform on which a concrete indigenous warrior is ensconced, who appears to be blocking traffic. He no doubt represents the proud *cacique*, chin held haughtily up and arm militantly extended sideways, leading his people in their struggle for the holy ground behind him. It is not difficult to go past the barrier though: up to the right and then a hard left, following the sign indicating the direction of the beach: PONELOYA 20 KM.

Driving from León to Subtiava, you do not suddenly enter another world. The transition is gradual. The houses become simpler and smaller, there are fewer cobblestones in the road, and more and more of the women staring at you from doorways, have straight black hair and coppery skin. I detect an aura of distrust in their eyes, but don't give too much credence to this impression. After all, I only know one woman here, Emérita Berríos. When she showed me around her community, regarded as the keeper of Nicaragua's indigenous heritage, I did not notice a hint of mistrust.

She had introduced me to Esteban Bárcenas.

The field of gravel in front of Saint John's church is deserted. I head south on a dusty road full of potholes, tufts of grass and stones. Bárcenas' house is four and a half blocks away. The cobblestones have disappeared. Every now and then I have to jump over a stream of muddy kitchen sink water.

Sitting behind the doorway mending clothes on a Singer sewing machine, a man sees me standing in front of the open gate and beckons me to come inside. He shows me to a rocking chair. Through the back door he walks to the inner courtyard, where two women are doing the laundry.

A mint green wall divides the room in two parts. Presumably, there is a bedroom behind it. Against the partitioning wall is a table with a television. A clock in the shape of a large wristwatch is suspended above it. Over the door leading to the patio hangs a Virgin. Underneath it, an old man now shuffles inside bare feet. A threadbare pair of trousers is tied around his waist with a drawstring. In his wake a girl enters the room followed by the man who let me in. She sits on the table and turns on the television. The man introduces me to his father, Esteban Bárcenas, and takes his place again behind the sewing machine.

Bárcenas takes a seat in the rocking chair opposite me.

"Times are hard for Subtiava," he begins, looking at the children playing outside on the patio with a calm expression on his face. He runs his fingers through his graying hair and plucks at the cowlick sticking up in the middle of his head, that lends him a youthful appearance, reinforced by his lively eyes, which he now fixes on me.

We will talk first and then he will show it to me, he says.

Without a trace of bitterness he explains that Subtiava has always been left out. Take politics for instance. What a load of hypocrisy! Politicians only listen at election time. Once they have been elected, they don't know you anymore. During the latest election campaign the subsequent president came to Subtiava. Bárcenas had buttonholed him.

"*Jefe*," he said to him, "if I support your party will you grant me an audience?"

"Any time you want," the candidate had replied.

Bárcenas wanted to show him the documents. And ask whether his council could get more influence on decision-making regarding the community. But he is still waiting for an answer to all his petitions for an audience. Nicaragua is a sham democracy. As head of the council you would expect to at least be treated with respect, don't you think?

That is not to say things used to be any better. Maybe a long time ago, when Indians still wore loincloths to shield their private parts and had feathers in their hair. Before the coming of the Spaniards. Ten thousand Chorotegas used to live in Subtiava at the time. They were astrologists and sun-worshippers. The Spaniards suspended a sun from the rafters of St. John's, intent upon luring them into their church.

"'There is your God', they said," according to Bárcenas.

Naturally quite a bit has changed over the course of the years. When he was a boy, there were still straw houses, the roads in even worse condition and public sanitation horrid. There is a little more civilization now. And Subtiava has grown substantially. According to the most recent census, there are some sixty thousand inhabitants.

"What we need is our own mayor," says Bárcenas, "the one in León cannot deal with our issues as well."

Having an own mayor would make it possible for Subtiava to alleviate its most pressing needs. A dire example is the unemployment among adult men. The collapse of cotton growing has drastically reduced demand for farmhands. The only ones still working are the ones with professional training. Teachers, a couple of doctors, the odd lawyer. Women get by selling fruit and vegetables at the market.

"And the men?"

"They're at home enjoying the peace and quiet."

Bárcenas eyes me cheerfully. The men have made a virtue out of necessity: they do the household chores, they cook and bring the kids to school. Bárcenas thoughtfully scratches his lower arm. The slump in agriculture cannot be attributed solely to the cotton crisis any longer, he tells me. That was too long ago. The rains makes all the difference. Or rather, the lack of it. He himself has twenty *manzanas* of land. One of his sons takes care of it, but owing to the drought the crop has failed. He shrugs his shoulders.

"Subtiava doesn't produce anything. All people do here is consume."

He calls out to the girl to turn down the sound. Of course, life goes on, Bárcenas resumes, everyone does what he can. Except, at his age, it does not amount to much. But no matter, each man has his day. Fortunately, the council is not physically demanding. In this way, he is still able to serve his community. Things are moving step by step, but progress is being made. A local congressman has taken up their cause. That gives hope. H'm finally, finally…He stares outside dreamily. Yes, he would then be able to die with a clear conscience.

He will show it to me soon, he assures me.

The congressman wants to focus on Subtiava's bylaws. After all, they stipulate that in the spirit of tradition, authority is vested in a *cacique*. He is the head of a council of elders, who in turn have the power to take decisions on community matters. The bylaws date back to the beginning of the nineteenth century. Except, they have never been ratified. According to the congressman however, this will soon happen in parliament.

Bárcenas will believe it when he sees it. It's too early to be crowing victory. The past has taught him to practice patience. He tells about the revolution. Before their victory in 1979, the *guerilleros* had come to Subtiava with their tales of freedom. Thanks to agricultural reform, they said, the land would be returned to the indigenous inhabitants.

"Subtiava stood behind me," wrote one of the original Sandinistas, Omar Cabezas, born and bred in León, in one of the most famous novels about the Nicaraguan guerilla, *Fire from the Mountain*. He called a protest march in Subtiava "a march of Indians that marks the end of the exploitation of our people." Cabezas wrote that the spirit of the great cacique Adiact lived on in the spirit of Sandino.

"Like most other Nicaraguans we in Subtiava fought against Somoza's *Guardia*, because they were murdering our children," says Bárcenas.

But the Sandinista victory turned out differently than expected. For the first time, I can now see a trace of bitterness cloud over Bárcena's face. "What's all this about indigenous community?" said the Sandinistas. "We are living in modern times."

"And they went on to redistribute the land to their own people," says Bárcenas.

Times were hard in the nineteen eighties. Who doesn't remember the rationing? You barely got enough to feed your family. He turns up his nose mentioning the black sugar. You wouldn't even feed it to a horse.

Now that the war is over, the wealthy are showing up to reclaim their estates. Enrique Sánchez, a congressman from the Liberal party, has his two thousand *manzanas* of land back again. Sánchez lives near Poneloya, not far from Omar Cabezas, who caused a stir by chasing off two state civil servants with an M-16 because they had come to collect payment on an overdue electric bill.

Most of the land around Poneloya is uncultivated, Bárcenas complains. The agricultural cooperatives of yesteryear have been done away with.

"There's nothing left. No production, nothing."

He swats a fly from his cheek, watching the little creature buzz away and resumes talking.

"If the rains don't come soon, we're finished. They say it's because of *El Niño.* Still, the worst seems to be over."

He pauses for a moment. The look on his face brightens.

"Let's hope we then get *La Niña.*"

"And that's she's pretty," I say.

"And has blues eyes…," he replies with a lilt to his voice.

People on the street greet him politely. His friendly greetings in return exude authority. So too is the manner in which, his head bent slightly forward, he listens to what people have to say, and the way he takes his leave with a piece of advice or a witticism. Bárcenas tells me he is having a hard time walking. In the old days, he would leave the house at five in the morning and get to Poneloya by seven. Running the whole way. Now he can't even walk a kilometer.

Before we go to visit doña Ernestina, he wants to show me the Adiact museum, where the products of indigenous culture are on display. We are met by Ramón, a lawyer, who also maintains an office here. When the elders go to Managua, he is there to offer them advice. Ramón talks respectfully about the knowledge of the elders. He tells me they safeguard the survival of Subtiava's culture and tradition.

The museum consists of a hall and an inner courtyard. There are earthenware pots on the floor in the hall and tools made of stone and obsidian in a steel cabinet. Outside, Ramón points out the images of Gods, knee high blocks of stone with reliefs that are hard to discern. At the end of our visit, Bárcenas gives him a friendly tap on the shoulder and says thanks for the guided tour.

Ernestina Roque lives a couple of blocks away. Sand crunches under her slowly swaying rocking chair. Her chin lies on her chest. Deep wrinkles seem to crack her parchment skin and to vanish into her sunken cheeks. A girl walks over and gently nudges her awake. Startled, she lifts her head and stares wide-eyed. Bárcenas goes to sit beside her.

"We have come for the old papers, doña Ernestina," he says loudly in her ear.

Ernestina beckons the girl – a niece, Bárcenas tells me – who helps her to her feet. She shuffles over to a chest of drawers and rummages around a while before taking out a crumpled archive file. She shuffles back and hands the file to Bárcenas. He takes out a leather bound book, cautiously leafing through the thick pages.

"Here it is," he finally says handing the book to me.

The top edge of the musty sheet of paper he has turned to, is adorned with elegant flourished letters stamped with the seal of the Spanish Crown. The date of signature beside it is 1720. The letters represent the name of the governor of Nicaragua, who on behalf of the King of Spain, addresses himself to all the members of the municipality of Subtiava, declaring that the land adjacent to the community has been inhabited and cultivated by generation after generation of Subtiavans, and determining that owing to this circumstance rights ensue on the basis of which the Crown has decided to grant Subtiava ownership to the land of its forefathers. The following pages go into great detail describing the territory of Subtiava, supplemented with maps. The domain consists of a total area of sixty-three *caballerías* – nearly three thousand hectares – and extends to the sea coast at Poneloya. Enrique Sánchez lives there. Omar Cabezas does too.

"You see," Bárcenas says earnestly.

Everything goes one step at a time, Bárcenas tells me on the way back to his house. The next step is getting the statutes approved, then they will see how to proceed. The congressman wants to make sure that Subtiava gets its own mayor. The subject of land ownership has yet to be broached.

"And what about the papers?" I ask.

Bárcenas smiles affably and quotes president Somoza, who told his people in the nineteen forties: "You lost your land, because you don't have any balls."

Laughing, we enter his house. He motions I can sit down and takes a seat opposite me himself. After that rebuke, Somoza issued a decree calling for indigenous communities to stand up for their rights. In Bárcena's opinion he was a good president. Subtiava was granted five audiences under Somoza. The streets were improved, and so were the sewers. But that was a long time ago. No head of state has granted them a hearing since.

"And that's how it goes, step by step," Bárcenas says again. "That's just the way life is: you have to accept what comes your way."

Not that he is a pessimist. On the contrary. The future looks bright. Who knows what kind of upheavals the new millennium could have in store? He might yet live to see the day when he is the rightful owner to his ancestors' land.

"That would really make you the *cacique* of Subtiava," I say.

He has a good laugh at that. That's the way it used to be. When the Indians could run their own lives and had their own rights. In those days, the *cacique* ruled and decided over the community. But that has all disappeared with that whole blending of all those societies.

"I may very well be a cacique, but I cannot show my teeth too often."

He is silent for a moment before laying out his ideas. The earth is the wealth of the people. Everyone should be able to benefit from it. However, there are only a handful who profit from it. The capitalists. If you have money, you call the shots.

"Like the saying goes: 'With money, you can make the devil dance.'"

Fortunately, money is not the only way.

"Don't forget," he says slyly, "that the peasant is always aggressive. He goes for it and shoots those bastards. And if he doesn't have a rifle he uses his machete."

In silence we watch the girls who are playing outside. They are his grandchildren and great grandchildren. He himself has eight. It has been fourteen years since his wife passed away.

"No, no," says Bárcenas with a parrying gesture when I ask him whether he has remarried.

"I'm unfit for that sort of thing. At seventy-five, my time has passed."

When he was around forty, his doctor had told him that making love a lot would drive a man insane when he gets older. That is when he had cooled things down. On the other hand, a friend of his had just told him about a new pill.

"He said it makes you feel you were eighteen again!" Bárcenas guffaws, while flailing his lower arm up and down.

I can see he only has one tooth left in his mouth.

"The funny thing is," he says a little later while looking outside, "the older you get the more you resemble a child. You start drooling, saying strange things, have a hard time walking. And everything starts failing, your eyes, your head."

Then he turns to me: "There will always be children to take the place of us older people. That's how life goes on."

It is hard to make out the remains of a church in the half collapsed walls on the enclosed plot of wasteland. Vera Cruz is said to be the oldest church in Nicaragua. Bárcenas had told me it was just a couple of streets away. Somewhere under the rampant growth of shrubs must be the altar, where legend has it that on every White Thursday of the year, the tortured soul of the great cacique Adiact appears in the form of a Golden Crab to betake himself to his old dwelling place.

Just where Adiact lived, no one knows. But everyone is familiar with the place where he was hung. On the fence around the tamarind tree sit two men. They are watching baseball. Four players are having a game down the length of the street. I look up. The tree must be at least four hundred years old, because it was at the outset of the seventeenth century that the Spanish conquerors, fleeing a volcanic eruption, were granted land near Subtiava by Adiact. That's were they founded present-day León. This noble gesture would prove fatal to the great cacique. His fair daughter Xochitl fell in love with a Spanish captain and brought down the wrath of her indigenous fiancé. Out for revenge he spread the rumor among the Spaniards that a revolt was brewing in Subtiava. The Spaniards did not hesitate and set a terrifying example for the people: Adiact was strung up from this very tamarind tree.

The men tell me people take bets on baseball games. For fifty *córbodas*. Or a hundred. Not them. All they do is watch. Enjoying the shade of the tree.

On the way back to León I stop at the concrete statue of the Indian. It is twelve noon. The sun burns directly overhead. A little further on two men are sitting in the shade. They gesture that I should go back and keep on going straight. To the beach. I shake my head and point to the city. I am going to see professor Buitrago, the old history professor, to talk about his city of León. "Nice stories," he will tell me, "good for the identity of the Subtiavans, but downright fabrications. Adiact never existed. His legend was dreamt up by one of our romantic poets not a hundred years ago."

I wander around the small trench surrounding the statue, examining the pedestal and the concrete body. Not a name in sight. A small canal to the back of it discharges into a pond, which just like the trench and the canal is dry as a bone. Rays of sun ricochet off the white tiles. Squinting in the harsh sunlight I see Bárcenas hand me the book. The papers are real. I had them in my hands.

"This is the official proof," he said.

THE SORCERER OF MASAYA

F AM. GARAY. The sign hangs on the fence next to the entrance of a sandy yard full of trees. Under a lean-to are three pool tables in a row all covered with plastic tarps. From the doorway Carlos Garay invites me to come in with a wave of his hand. He shows me to one of the rocking chairs, all set neatly in a row and takes another one for himself. It is early. The first client has yet to come.

I have read about him in *El Nuevo Diario*, the juiciest newspaper in Nicaragua. Drunken fathers who hacked their whole families to death with a machete, girls who put an end to their lives with rat poison after losing the love of their lives, attackers who raped and killed their victims, all vie for attention on the front page. *Curanderos* are a hot item too. The newspaper reports one miraculous cure after another. 'Little boy saved in terminal stages of cancer, 'Man regains eyesight after years of being blind', 'Women freed from the devil.' Carlos Garay has made a name for himself as an exorcist. People from all over the country find their way to his house in Masaya.

Garay looks at me bright-eyed behind the dark tinted glasses with gleaming metal rims. A cigarette dances to the rhythm of his rapid hand movements accompanying his stories about the past. At seventeen he went to New York. He lived there for two years. In Queens. Johnson Boulevard. Garay worked in a furniture factory. You made good money, but it was a hard life. Especially, being on your own. Carlos struck up a friendship with a Colombian minister of a Seventh Day Adventist church and paid house visits to *Latinos* with him. The Colombian was a healer and Carlos became his assistant.

"That was better than staying at home in your apartment all by yourself."

A year later he relocated to Miami. A beautiful city, good climate, and practically everybody spoke Spanish. He had lived there for nine years, when immigration refused to renew his residence permit upon his return from a vacation in Nicaragua. Carlos concocted a story that he had two children in the United States. To put pressure. But the Yankees saw through it. He laughs. Considering that all he was ever officially issued was a thirty day visa, he had managed to hold out for quite a long time!

Back in Nicaragua he sided with the Sandinistas. A logical thing in the mid-nineteen eighties. After all, you could not do anything if you were not on their side. He served in the army and became a police officer. In this official capacity he had jurisdiction over the market in Masaya. That is how it all began. One day a market woman came to him to complain that her husband had overturned her market stall and poured water and salt all over her – an evil omen. Carlos made a report of the offence. That was all he could do. But the woman kept on insisting that he could help her. The surprised Carlos figured that maybe she was mixing him up with a friend, the *curandero* from Tisma. The woman was ready to pay right then and there and so they went to visit his friend. He told Carlos: "Sorcery is your thing." Carlos had never really given it much thought, but his friend insisted: "You are going to cure her." He then pointed to a spot in the yard and said: "If you're a man, you will dig there." Carlos dug a hole one and a half meters deep and came across a book. A sorcerer's book.

"That woman was my first patient."

Not that he had become a *curandero* that first day. It was not as simple as that. It took him a while to get up to speed. Via via. It made sense, since the Sandinistas were against anything that smelled of the supernatural. The police could pick you up for it.

"And what about you then?"

"I was a policeman myself."

He has been able to devote all his time to sorcery for years now thanks to the transitional president Violeta Chamorro. She eased the reins, absorbed as she was in her struggle to restore peace in Nicaragua after all those years of civil war.

"Doña Violeta needed us," Carlos explains. "When the Sandinistas lost power, the international brigades and the Cubans left. They included thousands of physicians. And the government had to downsize, cuts were also made in the health care sector. We came to plug up these holes."

Carlos wants to show me his work space. I follow him through the living room into a little hall, on the other side of which he holds open a door. I step into a small space with bare walls of concrete. Carlos follows me in. We go to sit at a table beside the bed, a wooden plank on legs with a blanket over it. Carlos lights up a cigarette. He tips the ash into the bowl on the table, in which there is a green globe the size of a soccer ball. At the foot of the bed is another small table with the same kind of globe, among earthenware saucers filled with incense ashes and candle-grease. There are two small Buddha's under the table. Carlos clears his throat and spits on the ground. He hands me a well-thumbed book. The book he once dug up. It is filled with prayers to counteract all sorts of evil. I read about magical rituals, their attributes and directions for their use. The *Infernal Book* dates back to 1001 and was written by Johan Sulfurino. It was inspired by the life and works of Saint Cyprian, a Persian magus who became a Christian out of the love for a woman and was eventually declared a saint. Carlos holds up a more recent edition, the one he uses. Actually there is no secret to his sorcery. He taps the book. It has everything. He leafs through it and hands it over to me.

"These prayers are used to exorcise the devil."

I take a look at a long series of prayers, all of which begin with the words "I, servant of God", and in which God, the devil, Lucifer, the archangels and Satan are summoned to banish the demons to the realm of shadows.

But that doesn't mean everyone can become a *curandero*, Carlos continues. Friends who saw him in action and said "we can do that too, it looks easy enough," ended up on his bed all too soon. They had become victims of the power of darkness. You never know how things can end up anyway. When Carlos told his friend from Tisma that he was conducting exorcism of demons, his friend told him he had never dared to do that. Too dangerous.

"But I do it," Carlos simply says.

The most hopeless cases pay him a visit. They snort and they drool. Some of them are so wild it takes four men to hold them down. In order for a session to succeed - more often than not you have to come back every day for a week - people readily pay the equivalent of three months wages of an average Nicaraguan. But it is money well spent, says Carlos, for when it comes to the spirits he is always successful. He raps on the book again.

There are other books of prayer too. He shows me a couple of them. However, none of them contain prayers to exorcise demons. The *Infernal Book* is all the more special since it is not reprinted any longer. He just happens to have an extra copy. From a man who asked him to sell it for him. Carlos takes it out of a briefcase and puts it in my hand. One thousand *córdobas*. I lay the book on the table and leaf through the other prayer books. You have prayers to the Holy Marta, the armadillo, the just judge, the shadow of Saint Peter, the lemon, the Lonely Soul. Most of them deal with people's love lives. The great majority of clients come here for that, Carlos says shaking his head.

"How much evil in this world is not wrought in the name of love."

Other *curanderos* go so far as to call for the death of the mistress of an adulterous husband, but not Carlos. He does not put a curse on anything. That is black magic. He deals in white magic. To neutralize curses. Every evil has its counterpart.

"But what is good for one person, might be bad for someone else," I suggest.

Carlos shrugs his shoulders.

"I just do what the client asks."

And the client does what he asks. Recently, there was a woman who wanted her husband back. He gave her a jar. She had to put something of her husband's in it – a lock of hair, a fingernail, a photograph, an article of clothing, anything that contained a bit of his energy – and then bury it in the backyard. Garay ordered her to masturbate over it at the stroke of midnight while thinking of the devil with all her might.

"She did. And her husband came back."

Curing people is more difficult for him. It is not his specialty. Whenever someone is ill he therefore tries to ascertain beforehand whether or not a curse is involved. If that is the case, he proceeds. If not, he refers someone to a hospital or a pharmacy. Others do not do this, they take everything that comes. And so he does not agree to what people say, that Nicaragua's "cradle of sorcerers" is situated in the white villages. Diriá, Diriomo, Niquinomo, Catarina, are reputed places, but in Garay's opinion, with the deceased Juan Castellón they have lost the last of their great *curanderos*. The only thing you have left are the quacks, who live off the glory of their predecessors.

For a moment, he contemplates in silence.

"But hey, Nicaraguans just love lies," he resumes, widening his eyes at me at now. "They want to have the wool pulled over their eyes. Even if they have some perfectly treatable ailment, they would rather hear it is the work of the devil."

A woman comes in saying that the drunkard is here. Show him in, says Carlos. The woman leaves the room and a little while later a man enters, who looks to be around twenty-five. He sits down on the bed.

"Isn't it over yet?" Carlos enquires.

"I'm afraid not."

"Well, then it looks like you've got a pretty bad case of it. Lie down and close your eyes."

He picks up his infernal book and takes a little red pillow out of his trouser pockets, which he puts to his patient's forehead, pressing it down firmly with his right hand. Then he starts reciting, so inarticulately fast that I can only get the last word: 'Amen.' From a little plastic bottle he sprinkles, or rather pours water over the man. His face contorts, he breathes hard. Carlos makes the sign of the cross above his forehead and across his chest and stomach. Then he taps him on the chin, and the man opens his eyes.

"You took a nasty blow, didn't you?"

The man nods.

Carlos gives him a towel and while the man rubs himself dry, he explains to me that this patient is suffering from dipsomania. You can suppress it with treatment, but after awhile it starts all over again.

"Imagine, this man has to work for a living, but once he gets on a roll, he stumbles through Masaya night after night in search of booze. Without sleeping. How long has it been now?"

"A couple of weeks," the drunk replies.

The man tells of the little white monkey that appeared in his house again, just before his last attack. Carlos looks at me with a twinkle in his eye.

"Witchcraft, you understand?"

He asks the man to keep the faith and come back in four days. The man says goodbye and walks out of the room, after which the same woman appears in the doorway to announce the next visitors.

"Let them in," says Carlos, who hands the woman the little plastic bottle asking her to refill it.

"What's in it?"

"Holy water."

"How do you come by it?"

"Everyone can make holy water," says Carlos gripping an imaginary bottle, making the sign of the cross and saying: "In the name of the Father, the Son, and the Holy Ghost. Like this, you see."

The woman brings back the refilled bottle. She puts it on the table next to Carlos and leaves the room again. A couple now enter. Carlos asks the wife how things are going. The last treatment helped to ease the pain, she says, but she is still not rid of it.

"If you want, we can go further," says Carlos.

She emits a little laugh. Of course she wants to.

"I'll do anything to get rid of that rheumatism."

The woman lies down on her back. While reciting prayers, Carlos takes her right shoulder between two fingers, pinching hard, and letting go with a jerk. He slings water at her ankles. The husband, who is standing near the door, mumbles along with the prayers, and ends with Carlos: "Amen."

They will come back in four days.

The next patient is a big girl who looks to be about seventeen. Her mother has come with her. The girl sits down on the bed.

"Did you rub it in like I told you?" Carlos asks.

She nods gravely, adding timidly: "But it hasn't helped much."

Carlos gives her a fatherly pat on the shoulder.

"You mustn't think you can get rid of him just like that, sweetheart."

He tells me, it's about another *curandero,* who makes her dance in a circus. There is an appalled look in his eyes. In bikinis!

"Go on," says the mother, "tell him."

"What sweetheart?" asks Carlos.

The girl fidgets with her hands and says the *curandero* has threatened to put a curse on her house if she stops dancing. Carlos pauses to consider, looks at the mother and then at the girl.

"Lie down," he finally says to her and begins reciting.

The mother mumbles to no one in particular that it had all begun years ago, when she herself had started having problems with her husband.

Carlos wakes the girl with a tap on the chin.

"You had a blow, didn't you?"

She nods.

He asks them if they go to church. The mother no longer goes since those problems with her husband. Carlos thinks it's a good idea for the women to start attending mass again. He gives the girl words of encouragement. She should not be scared. Keep on rubbing it in. And come back in four days.

"How does the church stand concerning your profession?" I ask Carlos when the ladies have gone.

"The church has no objections," he answers.

The Bishop of León had recently said in a reaction to Carlos curing a girl, that anyone who trained to do so, could become a healer. Moreover, all he has to do is show the prayers to any client enquiring about his faith to make clear that he is working with God's blessing.

"A *curandero* is actually a mediator," Carlos explains, "an instrument. You cannot heal someone if it is against God's will."

He does not have a high opinion of the church. Even though he was baptized a Catholic and occasionally attends mass, Garay considers himself an agnostic.

"Read what it says in the Bible and compare it to what they do in church: worshipping saints and virgins. According to the Bible it is wicked, but there isn't a priest who forbids it."

Carlos dislikes priests most of all.

"Celibacy does not amount to a hill of beans," he says with disapproval.

How many women haven't cried their hearts out to him? The spiritual suffering is great when the priest puts his hand under your dress. Not to mention the afflictions suffered by men.

Carlos adheres to his own reading of the Scriptures. Jesus and the apostles were *curanderos*, just like him. How else could they have performed such miracles? The saints are cut from the same cloth. And the greatest sorcerer and devil worshipper of them all, was of course St. Cyprian.

The woman appears in the doorway again. She lets in a man who looks about thirty. He says hello, sits down and jumps right in: "Now she wants to get a divorce."

He heard it from his mother yesterday, who had heard it from a girlfriend, who had in turn heard it from another girlfriend, who is a friend of his wife.

"And you still want her back, don't you?"

"Sure thing."

"Do you already know who the other person is?"

"No."

"Try to find out, so we can do something about it. And now first lie down."

After the treatment the man takes a sheet of paper from his pants pocket and hands it to Carlos. There is a prayer on it to get her back.

"I figured: let me show this to Carlos. After all, you're the expert."

Carlos gives him back the sheet of paper.

"Ok, let's hear it."

As the man reads it aloud, Carlos gives me a bemused look.

"It sounds fine," he interrupts the man, "the most important thing is that while reciting the prayer you think as strongly as you can about your wish, that is, that you want her to come back to you."

"Shall I go on reading?"

"No, it's ok, that's enough."

The man folds the paper again and puts it back into his pocket. He now turns his attention to me. How his life has changed ever since he found himself with Carlos!

"I was down and out. No job. Hardly any clothes left. A pair of gym shorts was all I had on. And then all that misery with my wife."

With both hands he lifts his checkered shirt by the thumb and forefingers and then pats his smart pair of blue jeans.

"And just look at me now."

Following Carlos' instructions he had found the sack of salt and urine under his bed. Something else had to be going on.

"A *curandero* feels these kinds of things," Carlos says.

Thanks to Carlos he has been able to get his life back on track, the man continues saying. In the first place, he owes him gratitude for not charging anything for his services as yet.

"I didn't have a cent and Carlos said: 'We'll take care of it later.' When the time is ripe, he'll be the first to be paid."

All indications are that it won't be long. Work is starting to come, nothing really solid as yet, but you can feel it, people are starting to pay him visits again. What would Carlos think of him selling books door-to-door? It doesn't sound like a good idea to Carlos.

"Listen," says Carlos, rummaging three candles out from under the bed. "I'm giving you these candles to take with you. You turn them over..." One by one he bites off the bottom end, spitting out the candle-grease. "You smear them with ashes and sugar and then light them, at twelve midnight, if you can..." Carlos lights the candles and gets to his feet. "...and you hold them up. Think about your wish, that she would never be able to live without you, and jump three times, one..." Carlos jumps. "...Satan! Two," Carlos jumps. "...Lucifer! And three..." Carlos jumps. "...Luzbel! Then you stick the candles in the ground and let them burn down."

The man asks if he can have some paper so he can write this all down. He wants to follow the instructions as closely as possible. Carlos gives him a sheet of paper and waits until the man has finished writing.

"And one other thing," he continues, "for next Sunday. Fill a tub with water and put it in the yard. Then go and stand in it, naked."

"Naked?"

"Do it late in the evening, around midnight, it should be fine then. Take your oldest t-shirt and tear off the right sleeve over your head."

"Wait a second," says the man busily writing it all down, "the right sleeve, you said?"

"I'll show you how."

Carlos takes off his shirt and pulls the right sleeve over his head. "You pull it down and then you say: 'Satan, take your portion and go away!'"

"And the water?"

"You must throw it away. The t-shirt too. Put it out in the garbage."

The woman appears and announces that "the girl" is here.

"Almost done," says Carlos.

He asks the man to come back and report to him in four days time.

When he has gone, Carlos gives me a serious look. The girl is possessed by the devil. The treatment has been going on for a couple of days already, but he has not been able to catch the demon. Today perhaps.

"I'm afraid you're not allowed to be present here. Not that I mind, but I have to think of my clients. I know them. They don't want outsiders around."

He gets to his feet. I follow him out of the work space. There is a couple waiting in the living room with a girl of around twelve in between them. The parents grin sheepishly. Garay greets them like old friends. The girl, a plump child with bulging eyes, stares blankly around. Garay gesticulates they should move to his work space. The parents take their child by the hand. She starts snorting and kicking up a big ruckus. Carlos walks behind them and shuts the door.

The living room is left behind deserted. I go and sit in a rocking chair and listen to the drone of the refrigerator against the wall leading to the corridor. On a desk in the corner near the window is a sign with big, red letters. THERE WILL BE A CHARGE FOR EVERY CONSULTATION. On the wall behind the desk hangs a clock like the one at Estebán Barcenas' place, an enormous wrist watch. I detect a connection between the ticking of the watch and drone of the refrigerator, as if the ticking was keeping time to the drone.

Carlos' voice resounds. Unintelligible sounds are strung together in a series of rapid utterances, monotonous and incantatory volleys, that Carlos emits with a gradually swelling crescendo of higher pitched and louder vocal strains, culminating in a grand finale of one last exclamatory outburst. "God Almighty!" he screams. Then silence. Faintly, I can hear the girl moaning, but Garay resumes and his words are swishing high and hard throughout the house again. One litany following another. In the intermittent silences the girl's moans are audible. Now Carlos calls out: "Angel Michael", then "Satan!" or "Lucifer!" The girl screams and whines.

After a momentary silence, the treatment room door opens. Carlos comes into the living with his sleeves rolled up. He sits down next to me. Beads of sweat pearl on his forehead. A short break. The pain is in her back, he explains, precisely where the devil has lodged.

"The beast began to scream and spit. This is a curse that has been following the family for years. I am not finished with it yet."

He daubs his forehead with a handkerchief and leans back.

"Listen," he tells me a little later, getting back to his feet, "I have an idea. You come along and tell them you are my assistant."

"Fine with me."

"Besides, she is so wild we can use and extra pair of hands."

I follow Carlos into the treatment room. The girl is lying on the bed. She appears to be asleep. Sitting at the foot of the bed, her mother and father regard her with concern. There is also a young man present. Another assistant? I mutter a hello and mumble the explanation we agreed on. Nobody pays any attention.

Carlos asks us to hold on to the girl's arms and legs. She resists. He leans over her, speaking words of encouragement. She looks back with fear. Garay spreads his hand over her forehead. Slowly his fingers glide down and close above her nose. He takes his hand away and shoots out his fingers. Then he takes the little red pillow, puts it on her forehead, pressing down firmly with his right hand. With the other hand he grabs the *Infernal Book* and begins: "I, servant of God…"

He pours a bottle of holy water over her face. The girl squirms. Then he sprinkles her belly. She screams and tries to break loose from our grasp. Garay starts a fresh prayer. Now his right hand is moving to her lower back. He plants his fingers around the area of the kidneys and pinches. The girl screeches and wrestles. We grasp her even tighter. Garay squeezes again and again. The girl yells and writhes. There is a remarkably great deal of power lurking in her young body. Garay spews prayers over her in wave after wave. He has grabbed a cross which he holds before her face. Now he too is screaming. He is foaming at the mouth. The girl twists her body, kicks and arches her back.

Then Carlos collapses back in his chair, and is silent. The girl relaxes. Her screeches turn to whimpers. Father and mother bend down over her, stroking her face and speaking to her lovingly.

"I still haven't been able to catch him," Carlos says, panting. "I've haven't got any strength left today. We'll carry on tomorrow."

The parents stand there looking as if the memory of a horrible, incomprehensible nightmare, from which they have just awoken, is still lingering inside them. The father turns towards me.

"Really," he says, "before I came here I didn't believe in this kind of thing."

His wife backs him up.

"It is incredible," she says.

All of us walk outside. The parents try to reassure their child by telling her it will all soon be over. The girl looks around with that glazed look in her eye again. The words do not seem to be making the slightest impression on her. Carlos accompanies them to the door.

"One more day, maybe two, but then she'll be back in order," says Carlos, after both of us have sat down in a rocking chair.

He looks around the empty living room.

"Take a look at how many clients. Not a single one!"

Carlos shakes his head with displeasure.

"Do you know how it works in Nicaragua when you start a business? At first, it's booming, but after a while everybody packs it in and they stop coming."

That is why he has put the pool tables in the yard. In the afternoon they take off the tarps and by evening the place is reasonably full. Luckily, he also has a taxi cab working for him. But hey, things are getting more expensive every day. He raises his eyebrows.

"You have to do what you can do to make ends meet."

Two women appear in the doorway.

"The possessed one from Nindirí," Carlos whispers to me. "Last week her mother brought her in. She could not speak and saw blackness all around her. Raving mad."

He gestures for them to come further.

"What a difference a week can make, am I right?" he says.

The woman he spoke to nods. The other one says that her daughter's husband has returned home. She is almost her old self again.

"Satisfied customers," Carlos smiles at me.

He does know that his neighbors do not take him very seriously. Ah, that's what it says in the Bible too.

"You cannot be a prophet in your own land," he says, getting to his feet.

We say our goodbyes. His visitors desire his attention.

FAITH

Diriamba. A run-of-the-mill town. The kind of town you notice just as you are about to leave it. A church, a square, a boarding house and a couple of streets. Streets that run in a straight line from north to south and east to west, in which only the memory of a colonial look braves the wind forever blowing on the Nicaraguan tableland. Even the dust from this dry and barren country is swept away. Sounds scatter. And illusions.

It is dusk. On the way to Diriá, one of the sorcerer's towns, I have taken the wrong bus and ended up in Diriamba. Bar *Flomoli* is the only place serving a meal.

"Hello, my friend," a man calls out as soon as I have taken a seat.

"Hello."

"How are you?"

"Fine, and you?"

The short, slight man gets to his feet and totters over to my table. He bows forward and extends his hand.

"Please let me introduce myself: José Hernández, at your service."

His breath smells strongly of alcohol. The man sits down and stares straight at me from his watery eyes.

"Do you speak espanish?"

"Yes, I do."

His gaze remains fixed on me, he takes a puff from his cigarette and exhales.

"Fine then. Spanish it is. That's easier. And better. That way we can understand one another well. It is important for people to understand one another, am I right? Let's talk, that's what we're here for, aren't we?"

Hernández clears his throat.

"I'd like to ask you a question. Just one. See if you know."

He restrains himself.

"We're sitting here, peaceful, having a chat. That's great, isn't it?"

Again, he waits.

"But all the same, and that's what I want to ask you: where is the faith?"

"The faith?"

"Yes, the faith. What is the faith? You look like you have been to school, you're intelligent if you ask me, that's why I'm asking you, because it's pretty complicated. Do you know what faith is? Can you explain that to me? Just that."

He brushes back a lock of hair from his forehead and keeps on looking straight at me, until the cigarette falls out of his mouth and he bends over to pick it up. He puts the cigarette back and awaits my reply.

"Faith," I say, "that is believing in something without knowing what it is, believing that the road you are following is the right one. Something like that."

"Exactly! Something like that. But you don't know it, not really. I don't know, no one knows. No one can explain to me what faith is. Where is it? I'm telling you, right, I tell you: faith does not exist."

With a sluggish, but sudden movement, he turns around and waves his arm into the air.

"*Señorita, señorita*, please bring two more beers. You do want to have a beer with me, don't you?"

"But, aren't you a Catholic?" I ask, after we have toasted.

"You bet. Yes, I'm a Catholic. I believe in God and I go to church."

"And the priest, what does he say?"

Hernández shrugs his shoulders.

"He can't tell me where faith is. He doesn't know either. And let's be honest, what does faith have to do with me going to mass, where I think about the Lord and only see women. I pray and meditate on Him, as deeply as I can, you understand, and the only thing I see are women, naked women. How can you say you are a believer then? When all you can think about during mass are women?"

"Faith and women are two different things, aren't they?"

"Faith doesn't exist, I tell you…I'm in my fifties, right, so we might suppose I have a little more experience than you, shall we say, about the things of life."

He tosses back his beer, froth spews out of the corners of his mouth. With the back of his hand he wipes his lips from left to right.

"You see, I have a garage, a couple of streets from here. I work every day, the way it should be. I have a wife and five children. But like I said: faith does not exist."

José shakes his head.

"How could that be if your favorite son dies? Of all my children, I had six you know, he was the one I loved the most. The best of all of them, right, that's what I told him, and then he dies. What good is faith, when it comes to those kind of things?"

He gives me a questioning look with his red-rimmed eyes, before staring down at nothing in particular.

"And that's when I started drinking. For at least a whole year, downing shots, morning, noon and night. I was still going to work, mind you, but all day long, although slightly less in the morning. Hey, *señorita*, two more beers please!" he shouts behind him, before continuing.

"You ask yourself, what did I do wrong? How was I supposed to know he was on drugs?"

He lifts up his head and looks me right in the eyes.

"Did you know I started having dreams? I saw the Virgin appear before me. Dressed all in white she was. As white as a sheet. I kneel before her and feel how she scatters leaves over my head, they turn out to be rose bush leaves. Then, a week later, a gentleman appears who is walking up ahead. I did not know it was the Son. Until he suddenly turned around. He points his finger in my direction and says: "You!"

Hernández jabs his finger toward me.

"A couple of days later my favorite son was dead. The best one, like I already said. He had planned everything. Suicide. What did I do wrong, I said to myself, right. Well, if this kind of thing happens to you, you ask yourself: where is faith? And during mass, when I want to be contemplating the Lord, all I can see are women. You understand what I mean?"

He downs a generous swig of beer.

"My workplace is doing pretty good, but you can't really make a comfortable living out of it. Sometimes my brothers and sisters have to help me out. They all live in the United States, you see. Four hundred, five hundred dollars. One of my sisters recently sent me a package. Do you know what was in it? Poison! To kill cockroaches, she wrote. But you kill cockroaches by stepping on them with your feet, bam and you're done! I don't need any poison, I need dollars. Well, the next time she comes to visit I'll make that perfectly clear to her."

He grimly takes another drag off his cigarette and throws it away.

"It all really sucks, I tell you. And busting your ass at the garage, even though I am really a flight engineer, right, but I couldn't get a job doing that."

He pauses briefly to reflect.

"Do you know what I say? Let's hope the new government is going to help the country get back on its feet. Don't get me wrong, I'm no fan of Somoza, but the Sandinistas have brought this country to rack and ruin. Under Somoza everybody had his job, and that was that. There was not as much mess with him as there was with the Sandinistas. What I'm telling you, if the new government does not help this country get back on its feet, we're all going to get screwed."

He stares down at his feet again in silence. Suddenly, he looks up at me.

"And you, what brings you here? Your work?"

"As a journalist."

He laughs.

"As a journalist. Well, you must be recording all this then? To put it in one of your papers. Fine. So let's tell the truth here, because that's what you should always do with journalists, tell the whole truth. And the truth is, what we were just talking about, right, the truth is that faith does not exist. Because you can talk and talk about faith without ever getting an answer. That is why I am personally telling you that faith does not exist. You don't know, nobody knows."

He calls for two more beers and says:

"I am very pleased to meet you, my friend. That's how you say it in English, isn't it? Pleased to meet you."

He lets a little laugh escape his lips, then turns serious again before staring back at the table.

"And I dreamt about the Virgin, scattering roses all over me, and the Son who said: 'You!' And then my favorite son dies, the best, you see? If I had known. For me, friend, faith does not exist. We're screwed, all of us."

He takes another big gulp, says nothing for a moment, and then resolutely sets the bottle down on the table top.

"Look, because you should always tell a journalist nothing but the truth, I am going to say something that is not very nice, but you mustn't put it in one of your papers, you understand. Something personal, between you and me."

He holds back, then looks at me askance.

"I don't know if I can tell you, I mean, it's really intimate, a question. Not nice at all."

The cigarette falls from his hands, but he doesn't notice.

"I am a full blown man, right. I have my wife and five kids… oh, I don't know."

He lights up another cigarette and raises his bottle.

"To your health, my friend, you are a nice guy. I can really talk to you. Because you are not from around here, you see."

He wipes the back of his hand across his mouth and lets his breath escape.

"Like I said, I'm a full blown man. Women appear before me, during mass, don't they?"

José looks me straight in the eye.

"But the truth, you want to know the truth, that's right isn't it? Nothing but the truth."

He takes a long drag off his cigarette. After another hefty swig of beer he leans forward, supporting himself with his arms on his thighs, loosely cradling the bottle in his hands. He looks at me out of the corner of his eyes.

"My wife…my wife, how shall I put it, my wife doesn't want to have anything to do with me. Like an iron bar, that's how she lays there. And I…I can't bear it. She has closed her legs on me for years now. And I just can't bear it, you understand?"

He sits up straight a bit, sizing me up with an intense, but blurry look in his eye.

"You, on the other hand, you see, as big as you are, I'm just some shrimp, but you look virile. At least, it seems like it to me. Am I right or what? She hasn't wanted to do it with me for years, but you…my wife could fancy a bit of that."

José goes silent, with a vacant stare, taking his time before speaking again: "Look, my house is two kilometers from here, two blocks south of the Colonia. When you go that way, you'll automatically find yourself standing in front a big white house. 'That's the most beautiful one around,' you will say. My house is the best one in the street."

He looks bashfully at me.

"I'm going to ask you an indelicate question…something between us, right. The thing is this. If you go with me, you will… you will find my wife…Me, like I told you, she hasn't wanted for years. But you. My wife, that is… she will give you a warm reception…with her legs spread wide open."

He stares blankly into space, takes a big swig of beer, staying still and lost in thought for quite some time. Then in a serious tone of voice, even though he is having trouble speaking, he says:

"And all I can do is think of women, even in the house of God, and those dreams, right, and my son, who dies. That's why I'm telling you, *amigo*, the truth, since, after all that's what we've been talking about all along, the truth is, faith does not exist."

That's the way it is. Diriamba. A run-of-the-mill town. Before the intersection, where the main road bends to the left and goes out of town past the gas station, is a church steeple. Just as austere as the surrounding fields, with a simple dial facing every direction of the wind. Slow and relentless the hands of the clock move, while the wind blows by, day in and day out, carrying dust, sound and illusions in its wake. Even faith, which surely does not exist here.

COSTA

BLUEFIELDS BLUES

O smany is waiting for me at the landing strip. That is, the man with the impeccable haircut – and a comb as the most prominent weapon of his Cuban charm – coming forward, makes himself known as Osmany. He walks ahead of me off the airfield, into the 'other' Nicaragua.

Half an hour after leaving Managua, it came into view. There lay the mountain ridges that divides Nicaragua in two from north to south. The small plane which I shared with ten other passengers, was leaving the *Pacífico* behind, the Nicaragua of the Pacific Ocean, the land of the lakes and volcanoes, of the Spanish colony, conquistadores and cathedrals, the land of the *mestizos*. Over the mountains we were flying into the *Costa Atlántica*. Right up to the coastline you cross over a bare landscape of hills, once covered in virgin rain forest, crisscrossed by rivers that feed into lagoons, which in turn empty into the Caribbean Sea. European pirates once scoured these coasts. Later on the British laid down the law. Here, on more than half of the country's territory lives ten percent of the entire populace. Growth comes from over the mountains. *Mestizos* move in to settle, in search of new agricultural land. By now they constitute a majority. Invisible, for the time being, because on the Costa people pride themselves on being indigenous Amerindians or blacks, and in silence, because the *costeño* prefers speaking English.

After a short walk we reach a wooden house. Osmany greets the two men sitting in the yard. One of them is Pizarro, with whom he mans the Cuban medical mission in Bluefields. Thanks to our mutual acquaintance Emérita Berríos, I will be able to stay there for a couple of days. The other one, an older man, with a tanned, copper-toned head and fiery blue eyes, says he is a fisherman. He neglects to mention his name.

The man asks if I'm hungry. When I say yes he hollers something unintelligible into the house. Shortly thereafter a woman appears with a plate of rice and beans. I take out the bottle of rum I have brought with me from Managua. The woman brings each of us a glass. There is ice in the house, says the fisherman. He asks the women to get some cola and in the meantime serves a glass.

The fisherman says he left his country during the exodus of the *balseros* in 1994. He must have drifted south by accident, I figure. After all, the average Cuban refugee set course for Miami.

Nicaraguan rum may not be as good as Cuban, says the fisherman savoring the aftertaste of the first sip, but life on the Costa isn't half bad. Fishing provides you with a pretty good income.

He has gotten photographs from Cuba. His son got married there. The photographs are passed around.

"Beautiful bride, isn't she?"

The doctors nod.

"Pity, though, she's a mulatto."

The doctors nod again.

"If only she would have been white…," says the fisherman shaking his head.

Bluefields is the center of Creole Nicaragua. You read that the city owes its name to a Dutchman, the sea pirate Blauwveld. Purportedly, he was the first to have established a European settlement on this coast in the seventeenth century. Before that, English, French and Dutch pirates had holed up in the lagoons along the coast from where they launched attacks on the Spanish galleons. When piracy was curbed, they switched over to trading and farming and imported slaves, most of whom came from Jamaica.

Bluefields is far from Managua, but any passer-by there knows how lively it is here. How the women dance to *socá*! *Latinas* are jealous of the long-legged *morenas* and afraid their men want more than their own short legs. But you are also warned. Blacks are unreliable. And lazy. About the only thing they do is smoke and sell weed.

I walk behind Osmany and Pizarro into the mission post on Bluefield's main street.

To the Creoles, the arrival of the Cubans in the early eighties was the umpteenth hostile act perpetrated by the Sandinista regime. After the turnover of power in 1979 they had watched how the revolutionary authorities had set up their cadres on the Costa with *mestizos* from the Pacific region. This was hard to swallow for a population group that had taken prominent places in the Bluefields hierarchy ever since American multinationals had settled on the Costa at the end of the nineteenth century to mine gold and cut timber. At the time of Somoza's ouster, Creoles had control over most of the key administrative and managerial positions. The arrival of the Sandinistas meant they lost their jobs, just like the imported American goods, that disappeared along with the multinationals.

The strong anti-imperialist tinted nationalism of the Sandinistas fanned an old distrust: that the Sandinista was a Spaniard and his revolution the latest attempt to colonize the Costa. And to make matters worse, Cuban help meant the Nicaraguan revolution was communist. When the Cuban doctors arrived in Bluefields, the fat was in the fire. Riots broke out, that could only be restrained by the brute force of police units from Managua. But it never did escalate into a serious conflict like that between the Sandinistas and the Miskito Indians.

The Cuban mission looks like it has had its day. In the reception room is a faded portrait of Fidel Castro and a frayed Cuban flag. Osmany shows me to the guest room.

I freshen up and step outside, into the *Caribbean*.

Black women with big backsides shuffle past, holding umbrellas against the sun. Or the rain. In Bluefields it rains at least ten months of the year. Old people rock in their chairs on creaking porches. Children run after wheel rims they are whacking along with sticks. The main street meanders like a ribbon through the city, parallel to the wide bay of Bluefields, which is really a lagoon, whose opposite shore empties out in the sea at El Bluff.

A sluggish busyness pervades the harbor. Bare-chested dock-workers are unloading sacks of cement and corn. A lot of men are simply hanging around. Talking loudly, drinking rum, waiting for some small job. But there is not much work to be had. You have to go to El Bluff for that. That is where the fishermen bring their catches of lobster and shrimp, most of which is shipped to Miami. The boats moored here make you wonder whether they would make it through such a voyage. Most of them would not, they are half underwater. A couple of boats still able to ply the waters are rusted through so badly, you ask yourself whether they will survive the next tropical storm.

Two motorboats are ready for Pearl Lagoon, but there aren't enough passengers yet. The boatswains are busy drumming up people to fill the available spots. They do not shrink from stealing each other's customers. They approach anyone passing by and as soon as somebody shows any interest, they pounce on him like dogs fighting over a bone. The waiting passengers patiently listen to the shouting back and forth. No one wants to give up his spot, not even for the rain, that is now coming down in buckets. Umbrellas pop open everywhere. Apparently unfazed, Indians paddle their wooden canoes filled with oranges to the quayside. I go and shelter under the overhanging roof of the harbor office and strike up a conversation with a black guy who has also sought refuge there. Does he know where I might score some marijuana, I ask.

"Hey, you just met the right person, man!" he says, baring his enormous front teeth. His well-filled black leather cap shakes to and fro on his head. "If you want to smoke, I can invite you, man," he says, after half-jokingly asking me whether or not I am some DEA agent.

No sooner than it began, the shower has stopped. One of the boatswains points to his boat, which meanwhile has practically filled up. He vehemently signals that the boat is about to depart. I promise the black guy to come back tomorrow, head for the dock and hop on board.

The boat sails swiftly down the Rio Escondido. It feels like we are touching the surface of the water only occasionally when we hit a wave. We come past Rana, from where you can travel to Managua overland. Many trees along the banks have had their trunks snapped in two. The telltale traces of hurricane Juana, that ravaged this coast a few years back, I suppose. To the left and right shipyards pop up with rusty fishing boats. And also, right in the middle of the river or in the mangroves, shipwrecked vessels. Were they simply abandoned there, or destroyed during the contra war?

After passing Kukra Hill and Haulover we sail into the lagoon. *Laguna de Perlas*. Pearl Lagoon. It sounds more picturesque to me in English.

The boat moors on the dockside of the village with the same name. I jump off board and walk down the sandy road running straight through the village. To the left and right are wooden houses on poles. Chickens are running around, cackling away. Horses graze undisturbed on the shoulder of the road.

It is Christmas Day. People have come here from far and near, from Bluefields, Corn Island or the United States, to celebrate the holidays with their families.

Girls in soft yellow or pink dresses walk past hand in hand, chatting away. There is an account from the nineteen eighties, when *contra* soldiers had kidnapped twenty-five girls from Pearl Lagoon, for their own enjoyment as the story goes. Only one girl would come back alive.

In their Sunday best, the girl's parents follow behind them. They are no doubt heading for church. The bells toll from a white church at the end of the street.

"Hello mister, where are you going?"

Two young women are standing on the porch of a house, where loud music is blaring. Not to church, I say, telling them I am just having a look around town before going back to Bluefields.

"Stay with us," one of them says, pointing over her shoulder to the house. "We can dance. And then we go. You can stay until tomorrow."

I don't feel like diving into a disco. They wouldn't mind having a drink at the sidewalk café next door either. It's around noon. Another hour before the boat leaves. When the ladies bring up the disco again, I tell them I have to be on my way.

The boatswain and two of his buddies are drinking beer in a bar overlooking the dock. Before we can leave, he has to go and find a passenger, he tells me. The boatswain empties his bottle and walks into town. I go and sit on the porch in front of the bar and wait.

"Hello there, you," says an old man.

He shakes my hand and comes to sit next to me. His name is Rafael Campbell, he says. He is a Miskito Indian, he continues, and lives in Awas, a half hour by boat from here inland. A Miskito speaks four languages, says Campbell. Miskito, Creole, Spanish and English. Sometimes white people come all the way to his village to learn Miskito. They learn everything about it, go back home "and then they make money."

It is silent for a while, before Campbell changes the subject. Nicaragua is a good country, he says.

"We have a land of freedom. Maybe where you come from, there is no freedom."

Bewildered, I look at Campbell. Not that long ago the Miskitos were fighting for their freedom against the Sandinistas. They too regarded the coming of the revolution as another form of Spanish colonization. But whereas the Creoles and Sandinistas had settled their differences without bloodshed, things had been different with the Miskitos. They had been living on the Costa for much longer and felt they were being banished, when forced to leave land they had inhabited for centuries in the name of

Sandinsta land reforms. The memory of their former kingdom of Mosquitia could also have played a part, even though it had been lost more than a century earlier, when the Americans chased the British out of the Costa and made it into a reservation, where Miskitos worked as laborers in a mine or rubber plantation.

A drunken woman stumbles out of the bar, a half full bottle of rum in hand. She starts talking to Rafael who motions her to keep moving. She strolls around in the middle of the street accosting the first man that passes by. Soon, they walk off together hand in hand.

"Look," laughs Rafael, "she goes with anyone. You could make love to her right here and now. But that is not what God has intended. A man should stay with his wife. In life you have to know what you want and follow your own path. If you first go here, and then there, and then somewhere else again, you won't get anywhere."

I wonder whether the boatswain has "gone there" too and so is not looking for a passenger at all. In any case, he is keeping us waiting. Every once and awhile one of his buddies sticks his head out from under the tarpaulin of a little boat on the wharf, from which the head of a girl also emerges from time to time.

A wind is rising, blowing a cloud of sand across the road. Rafael has gotten to his feet and has walked on.

Now Stanley is sitting next to me. He hails from Pearl Lagoon.

"Yeah, a nice place," he reacts less than glowingly when I tell him I think it's a nice town.

The people here make a living from the water, he says. Not by diving for pearls no, there isn't a pearl to be found in the whole lagoon. Lobster and shrimp, there's plenty of that.

"If you own a boat, you've got it made. Then you're your own boss and with a little bit of luck you may be able to buy a second one."

But Stanley does not have money for a boat. I must understand that he does not have any steady work. When a boat comes in, he lugs crates of soda pop to the bar, baggage to the hotel. He gets twenty *córdobas* for one job, ten for the other. Food is no problem here, you can always get fish or something. Money is for the extras.

"Yesterday I wanted to take my wife out, like you're supposed to on Christmas Eve, have a couple of drinks, go dancing, but who can afford that these days?"

He did not have any money to buy presents for his kids either. So they all went to bed early.

"In life, it's all a matter of time, you know. Tomorrow things could be better. That is time. You can't force things. You just have to wait for the right moment and then…bang!"

He punches his fist into the palm of his other hand.

"If you really want to make something out of this life, it's possible. Everything is ready and waiting, but you have to do your best, work hard, day and night, persevere. Maybe next year, you know."

While getting to his feet he wishes me a Merry Christmas.

A little before three o'clock the boatswain shows. We have to get a move on, he says, because he wants to get home before dark and it will take at least two hours to reach Bluefields. The wind has started blowing harder. Pelicans skim across the whitecaps ahead of us. He was not able to find his passenger. I figure: the girls of Pearl Lagoon. Maybe next year.

"Let's walk."

His black leather cap bobs back and forth to the rhythm of his gait. At the corner with main street he turns around and extends his hand to me.

"By the way, I'm Earl, Earl Kirkland, pleased to meet you."

Just like yesterday I bumped into him in front of the harbor office. We stroll past a succession of grocery and hardware stores, fruit stalls, bars and eateries as we make our way out of the town center. The wooden houses stand on poles, all the doors and windows are closed off by screens. You see holes in the dingy walls, worm-eaten window sills and flaking paint. Bluefields is a poor town. The rebuilding of the worst damage from hurricane Juana has done nothing to change that. The contrast with the glaring white church, towering above the surrounding low houses, is all the more stark. It has clearly received a new coat of paint. A black man is busy pulling weeds out of the tidy front lawn of the church.

"The Moravian church," says Earl.

A good dose of mission work would save the indigenous population from their barbarous world of mist, wrote Orlando Roberts, a Scottish merchant and travel writer, who traveled around the Costa at the beginning of the nineteenth century. Not much later the first Moravian missionaries set foot on shore. That was three centuries after Columbus, who in 1502 was the first European to land on the Costa. But he was quick to leave. Later attempts by Spain to colonize the region all came to a dead end in the impenetrable jungle or were beaten back by the warring tribes of Indians. The Costa finally fell into English hands. They were not out for subjugation, but trade. The saving of souls was left to missionaries like the Moravians, whose strict gospel preaching a hard working and virtuous life gained access to both indigenous Indian and Blackman alike.

We walk through a forest of paths, wire mesh fencing, corrugated iron roofs, rubber tires and free range chickens. This is a poor area on the outskirts of Bluefields, a neighborhood, as Earl calls it. The people living here are black. And as a black man you haven't got a chance, he says. Good jobs are for the *mestizos*.

"Them Spaniards are the worst fucking racists in the world, man," says Earl. "They don't let us."

Things stay pretty cool in Bluefields though, because Creoles get less heated than the Miskitos, says Earl.

"We smoke grass, you know," he laughs.

As long as he can remember the stuff has been arriving from the sea by the bale. In Bluefields, you can buy anything. Coke, ganja, crack. All Colombian. The transport routes run via the Colombian islands San Andrés and Providencia or through the closer Nicaraguan Corn Island. Newspaper reports regularly appear about hundreds of kilos floating in the sea after a pursuit by the DEA or the Nicaraguan navy. If the authorities get too close for comfort, the couriers dump the stuff in the sea.

"It just washes up," says Earl. "The Colombians throw it overboard, a fisherman hauls it in, or we just find it on the beach. We have always smoked. For free!"

He holds open a rickety gate for me. Strewn over the yard are car tires and parts of engines. A cackling chicken whizzes away in front of us. There is a rusty set of swings with a bent frame.

"And this is Henry Morgan, a friend," says Earl when we enter the house.

"Hello," Morgan grins from a worn-out sofa inviting us to come and sit next to him. Earl first takes a wad of newspaper out of his back pocket. He unfolds the paper and hands it to me. The weed feels dry, but smells good. Rolling paper isn't available, says Earl, who takes the stuff back to roll up. The thin wrapping of toilet paper works just fine. No filter, no tobacco. *Pure Colombian.*

There is a show on television. The gogo-dancers are 'hot' giggles Henry. Just like the Dutch soccer team, he adds.

Earl, who moistens the paper with the tip of his tongue, looks up.

"The *clockwork orange*, right?" he says, finishing off rolling the joint.

Holland plays the most attractive kind of soccer, on that the friends agree whole-heartedly. They should have become world champions a long time ago. Earl takes a deep drag off the joint and passes it over to me. It tastes good, mellow.

Once Henry has taken a hit and passes it on to Earl, he looks dreamy-eyed in my direction.

"I'm a Morgan, you know," he says.

He is probably referring to the buccaneer, Henry Morgan. Does he mean he is a direct descendant? Anyone leafing through the Bluefields telephone directory will find the name of Morgan, along with other illustrious names from the annals of seafaring. Drake, for instance. African names did not fit the British ideal of civilization. Blacks had to have real names. In the telephone book you also find the more modern Marylins and Elvisses. And how about Alka-Seltzer, after the local painkiller, or Yale, after the brand of lock?

Henry's heart however, goes out to the past. The first *brothers* were stranded here after being shipwrecked on the coast at the outset of the seventeenth century, he tells me. The Miskitos are actually a people of mixed descent between those *sambos* and the indigenous population. The Sambo-Miskitos developed into the most powerful people on the *Mosquito Coast*. They held sway from Guatemala to Panama. They were greatly indebted to their association with the British, who annexed the Costa to their empire as a protectorate in 1665. The Miskitos proved to be outstanding trading partners. They supplied tortoise-shells that were highly prized in Europe and received weapons in return, thus enabling them to establish their authority and dominate more than twenty other tribes. Their good relations with the English even left them with their own nation: the Mosquito Coast became the kingdom of Mosquitia. Descendants of the first Sambo-King Old Man were sent to Jamaica, Belize and even London to learn the lofty arts of royalty.

Pearls before swine, thought the merchant Orlando Roberts. The Scot railed against the licentiousness of the Miskitos. Their king is more attracted to the bottle and to women than the affairs of state. His subjects, Roberts discovers, are anything but noble savages. They steal with a vengeance, lie and cheat and enrich themselves trampling on their indigenous brothers. They exact tributes from subjugated peoples and trade other Indians as slaves. Nevertheless, Roberts sings the praises of Miskito hospitality. He gives an account of the many receptions, perked up, as befits courtesy, by the rum he served, that ended in Bacchanalias lasting for days.

"But them *sambos* live up north," says Henry, languidly looking up from his reveries and fixing his gaze on me once again. "Here, we're plain blacks."

I crack up with laughter. Not so much because his eyes are bloodshot, but because of their color, for they are unmistakable: bright blue. Henry doesn't know what to make of it and his questioning eyes nearly bug out of his head.

Suddenly, he looks a lot younger. There he is, a little boy around eight years old, holding on to the peg leg of a man with a red beard and blue eyes. They are on a ship. With the foot of his other leg the man lifts the lid on a wooden chest. There's a glint of gold in little Henry's big eyes. He looks up with pride, the man with the red beard gives him a covetous smile. Above his head flutters a black flag with a white skull.

Darkness descends and there is a party. The seamen leap around a fire and grab at the skirts of the dark women. A little way off stands a forlorn Henry, glumly looking at the man with the red beard. He watches him burrowing his head into the bosom of a black woman and turning for another swig from the bottle every now and then, being passed to him by a white man whom Henry doesn't know. The little Henry turns around and walks into the darkness.

He reappears in the mangrove swamps along the coast. Peering over the water at the break of day. Looking at him from the side, I can see he is graying at the temples. Henry is an older man now, giving light signals. There is a droning sound and a little later a motorboat appears. Henry watches dark shadows toss the package overboard. The motorboat at first backs up, then turns and disappears. When Henry has waded a few difficult steps towards the package, he stops and pricks his ears. Again a droning sound. The old Henry hurries out of the water and hides in the mangroves along the shoreline. He sees another motorboat appear. On deck are ominous figures in blue uniforms. They haul the package onboard. Henry dives for cover from the harsh glare of a floodlight. When he hears the engines roar, he gets up and sees a terrifying eagle on the stern of the boat, that raises out of the water as it accelerates away.

In broad daylight I spot Henry enter through the big doors of the white church with his head bowed. His slow paces follow the cadence of the bells tolling in the spire. The doors close behind him.

Now he is sitting – still – beside me on the sofa.

"Wow," I say, "then that must make you about Henry Morgan the Tenth!"

"You got it!"

We burst out laughing and shake hands.

"Another smoke?" Earl asks.

"Sure," Henry and I reply in unison.

While rolling the next one, Earl talks about his clients. They come to Bluefields from every corner of Nicaragua. Marihuana is not done at home, but far away it's cool. *Latinos* smoke as much as the blacks.

"Them Spaniards are fucking hypocrites," he says.

By the way, the authorities are just as bad. If you are to believe the newspapers, they crack down hard on drug trafficking. Drug seizures are front page news. Busted dealers are mentioned by their full names. But, Earl asks, how come he has never done any time? Apart from that one exception. But that was in Europe.

"Yeah man, I was in Europe, ten years ago. In Hamburg. They tell me it's a lot like Amsterdam."

He stops rolling and looks at me.

"Freedom, you know."

He clicks his tongue with contempt.

"Freedom in Nicaragua? Plenty, but you need money. And not be black."

His European adventure was not a fortunate one. Earl was able to arrange a trip to Germany. He made a few deals there and was busted. Without proper papers. First tossed in jail for a few months and then deported back to Nicaragua. He could hardly believe they sent him back free-of-charge. The three of us all have a good grin.

"The police here are in on the action just as much as we are," Earl continues. "They leave you alone in exchange for some stuff. Do you really think they don't know who I am in Bluefields? But nobody does a thing. Hypocrites, them Latinos."

After one last careful lick he finishes rolling the joint and fires it up.

"We blacks are cool," he says after a deep drag. "You smoke what you like. No problem."

They prefer smoking Colombian, like this shit. They only smoke Nicaraguan weed if the sea has not thrown anything ashore, but for the time being that won't be necessary. In a large scale operation the police and army had made a huge drug seizure two weeks earlier, but just as much disappeared in the sea. An estimated six hundred kilos. So, there's good times ahead, although it drives the price down. You have five pound bags, Earl explains, that cost four hundred *córdobas.* In turn he sells one gram bags for ten *córdobas* a pop. Life ain't half bad in Bluefields. Earl takes another deep drag and passes it to Henry.

"Just be cool."

Henry stretches out comfortably on the sofa.

"Just be cool," he concurs coughing, while the smoke leaves his mouth in a short series of puffs.

It used to be a lot better, says Earl. Mushrooms used to grow everywhere. They would eat twenty or thirty at a time. Man, you were flying all day long, he laughs.

"Remember Winston?" he asks Henry dusting off an old anecdote about a friend tripping his brains out on mushrooms, who went down the street stark naked.

"Should have seen them Latinos watching!"

Henry mentions yet another friend, who also went out into the street and stood on one leg for twenty-four hours.

"Like a heron!" he screeches with laughter.

You also got *floripundia* here, Earl goes on. They are hallucinogenic plants. You boil them in water and extract the sap. Now that's a trip, man. But you have to be careful. If you don't boil them with the calyx facing downward it's pure poison. A friend of his went blind, you know.

"It scared my guts," he says, bursting into an irrepressible fit of laughter. But that was quite some time ago.

"But it's good, man. See, that's why I say: "If you don't die, you get high!"

Back at the mission, Osmany asks me if I feel like going into town with him. There's a look of concern on his face. He has lost his comb. It is already after noon and he has not been able to fix up his hair yet. I tell him it does indeed look a little unkempt, but he doesn't see the humor in my remark.

We go from store to store. Not that there is any shortage of combs, but Osmany thinks they are all too crude, too delicate or too expensive. Finally, he finds an instrument to his liking. He asks the saleswoman if there is a mirror. The woman holds a hand-mirror in front of him, whereupon Osmany touches up his hairdo with the skill and meticulousness of a professional.

Much relieved, he goes outside ahead of me, swiveling his head with satisfaction. However, he overlooks the black man passed out in the street and almost stumbles over him. Osmany shudders. He tells me I have to watch out. They're all a bunch of freeloaders and thieves. Instead of finding work they get plastered or get stoned out of their minds.

At a safe distance he slows down, rubs his hand through his hair and pulls out his new comb.

COOL-CAT

The *Lynx* is three days late. Because it's Christmas, they say. But today it has finally docked. It's a whacking great ship, that is for sure. At least forty meters long. This beast looks like it will be able to swallow up the whole wharf in a single bite. Bluefields harbor pales to insignificance by comparison.

Delivery vans drive on and off the pier. Dock-workers stand in chains and pass sacks of cement, flour and corn from hand to hand that disappear into the hold of the ship. Crates of beverages are stacked on the deck. About ten men hoist the body of a jeep on the forecastle. Amid shouting, laughter, and huffing and puffing they finally succeed.

By ten in the morning the ship is loaded. Departure has been delayed by an hour, but nobody could care less. For the time being, no one minds that one of the two engines is not in working order either. Even if that means that the voyage will take twice as long and those prone to getting a queasy stomach are going to regret it on the open sea.

The passengers may now board. I walk to the forecastle and lean against the railing. Stewards are pacing back and forth across the deck, asking and answering questions, and so it appears, racking their brains to get everything shipshape. The video in the passenger's lounge has been switched on. A bicycle comes on board.

Even though this harbor is not exactly the kind of place where you would think of beginning a voyage around the world, a sailing is a sailing, so too in Bluefields. Those staying behind urge those on board to take care of themselves. Those departing, assure them they will.

The gangway is hoisted on board. Two seamen cast off. The ship's horn blasts. Water swirls. Calls can be heard back and forth amid the flutter of white handkerchiefs. Everything, the last words of advice, reminders if anything was forgotten, best regards, everything is finally drowned out by the deep growl of the engines. Someone throws a kiss. The beast breaks away from the pier. Is that already the smell of sea air?

No, for we still have to cross the lagoon. The *Lynx* anchors briefly again at El Bluff to take on more cargo. Then we cross through a narrow straits where the current from the lagoon collides with the sea surf. Violent waves smash against the rocks of El Bluff. The *Lynx* cuts through them like a knife. The surf turns into a gentle swell. The coast shrinks to the size of a narrow stripe. We are sailing in the Caribbean Sea.

"Lonely, or lost in thought?" the girl asks.

I had been stealing a look at her dark curls, that fall over her shoulders and black dress with a motif of red flowers. How long has she been standing here on the forward deck, just a few steps away from me? Half an hour, an hour? Should I tell her that I'm shy? She wouldn't believe me.

"In thought," I respond.

There is a mischievous look in her eye. She seems to have an idea of what I am really thinking, but does not mention it. Her name is Genoveva. She is seventeen and on vacation with a girlfriend.

"My parents think I am in León with my grandmother."

"And your grandma?"

"She won't tell."

She says this with the decisiveness of someone who cannot be fooled about anything. Genoveva comes from Diriomo, one of the white towns on the tableland to the west of Granada.

"A gorgeous town," I lie, "just like you."

With a routine smile, she accepts my compliment. She starts telling me about her boyfriend Matias. He comes from Germany and is thirty years old. They are going to get married next year.

She turns her head in the breeze and looks out to sea. The swell has turned into rough water. Great waves roll calmly towards the coast. When the *Lynx* descends into a deep trough and crashes on the surface of the water, we have to hold on tight. Both of us are soaking wet from the water that has come crashing over the bow.

"Scared?" I ask.

Genoveva shakes her head and scoffs at me. I am cold and ask if she would like to go inside with me. She prefers to stay awhile.

In the passenger quarters, it feels like the ship is moving up and down even more. Women are hanging out of portholes, puking. I go and sit down next to a Creole. It seems like she is asleep, but when I sit next to her she opens her eyes and smiles. We exchange pleasantries. All I get to know is her name and the place she comes from. Jessica, from Bluefields. She shuts her eyes again. I try to get some sleep too, but go back on deck when I start to feel sick to my stomach.

The captain stops me at the bridge. A man of few words. The old salt cups one hand over his eyes, pointing to the distance with the other one.

"Corn Island."

I don't see anything. Not even when I cup my hand over my eyes, nor when I climb up to the bridge. But the island is out there somewhere. Seventy kilometers offshore from Bluefields. Nicaragua's very own Caribbean pearl.

"How long?"

"Another two hours," the captain says.

I walk to the forward deck. Genoveva has disappeared.

"Corn Island," I say to the couple, arm in arm at the railing, and point in the direction the old salt had indicated.

"Where?"

"Somewhere there. Just heard from the captain."

Both of them have already been to Corn Island several times, says Sharon. It figures, since they both come originally from Bluefields. Alan however has been living in Washington for the past twenty-nine years. He would love to return. For Sharon, I think, who has kept on living in Bluefields.

At five thirty in the afternoon, the *Lynx* enters Corn Island's South West Bay. The Caribbean waves must be battering the shore on the opposite coast, but here in the lee of the island the water is calm. The limpid mirror surface of the water reflects the setting orange-red sun. The *Lynx* docks at the concrete pier where a long white beach with coconut palms begins. Corn Island Beach, I suppose.

Alan and Sharon say goodbye as they disembark. I just saw Jessica, but I can't make her out among the departing passengers. I walk onto the pier with Genoveva and her friend. Together, we are going to look for a place to stay. They have heard of *Pensión Morales*, supposedly not too far away.

Mister Morales has a clean looking house with a fan in every room. There are exactly two rooms left, one for the ladies and one for me. By the time we go out to get something to eat, it is already pitch dark. The beam of light from Genoveva's girlfriend's flashlight plucks shadows out of the darkness, transforming them into faces that show us to the way to the town center.

In restaurant *La Rotonda*, lobster is being served. We order beers that turn out to cost twice as much as they do on the mainland. But it has to be flown in from Managua, says the waiter. The same goes for most other foods and basic necessities. Corn Island is exorbitantly expensive. Genoveva and her girlfriend realize they have made a huge mistake and decide to sail back with the *Lynx* the following morning.

After dinner we go for a stroll along the sandy main street. Wolfgang, a nice but gawky sociology student from Salzburg, who we met in the restaurant, is strolling with us. The main street widens into a round plaza where people congregate under globes of light on electric chords hanging like wreathes on the encircling poles. We walk into a dance joint. Just after the entrance is a large refrigerator with beer and soft drinks. The bar. You have to go down a short flight of stairs to a covered yard where people are dancing amid white plastic tables with white plastic garden chairs. The music is loud. The DJ is playing a few sentimental Latin numbers and some reggae, but mostly *socá*, the music from Nicaragua's Caribbean. Dazzling African rhythms and stirring percussion alternated with a lively brass section and jangling organs. *Morenas* shimmying their shoulders and shaking their hips.

In the right corner, a table is free. Genoveva sits down next to Wolfgang and immediately launches into an animated conversation. No doubt about Matias, I suppose. I ask her if she wants to dance, but she shakes her head no. Then I try and start up a conversation with Genoveva's girlfriend, but it quickly leads to a dead-end. Bored, I stare at the dancing crowd.

All of a sudden I see her. She has seen me too and comes my way. An angel to the rescue. In a sparkling white dress. Jessica. I offer her a chair. From the corner of my eye I notice Genoveva looking. Her conversation with Wolfgang stalls. He looks back and forth at Genoveva and me. Jessica takes a seat. When she bends over to make herself heard, I see she is not wearing a bra under her dress.

"I can go with you tonight," she says.

I gasp with laughter. At Jessica's uncomplicated proposal. And to hide that I am flustered.

"Sure," I reply with feigned self-confidence.

She lost track of me when the ship had docked, she says. Me too, I tell her. Then she pinches my leg and asks if we should dance.

"Sure," I repeat.

On the dance floor Jessica introduces me to Nancy, a raving beauty. It must be obvious that I can't keep my eyes off her, because Jessica says: "Do you like my girlfriend?"

"She is very beautiful," I have to admit. "But I like you more."

When the song is over, we go to the fridge for a beer. Back at our table, Genoveva and her girlfriend get up. They are going, she says. Because of the noise. Wolfgang goes with them.

"Friends of yours?" asks Jessica, when they head for the exit.

"I met them on the boat."

When she has finished her beer, Jessica wants to leave too. Genoveva and her girlfriend are still near the exit. It seems like they have been waiting for us. Wolfgang has gone to bed, he has to get up early to catch a plane. The four of us walk into the darkness, the light bulbs strung around the plaza have been switched off. The girlfriends are talking softly up ahead, Jessica and I follow a few meters behind. In the lamplight cast from the disco behind us, I see Genoveva turning halfway around. She says that I have to be careful about diseases. Jessica shrugs her shoulders.

"You better watch out," says Genoveva, when we reach the boarding house. Jessica and I walk past her up the three steps that lead inside. When she lies down on the bed Jessica clicks her tongue with approval. Not bad by a long shot. A mosquito net. A fan. Still, she feels a little warm. A body covered with scars appears from under her white dress. From fighting, she explains.

"I used to be aggressive. But not anymore, I'm really cool now." She laughs out loud. "Don't you worry about a thing."

Jessica is twenty-two now. Her mother died ten years ago. Somebody put a spell on her, she says. She lived with her grandmother until she was fifteen. But that was unbearable, because her granny is a nasty old woman. So she chose to take care of herself. She met a Nicaraguan dealer with whom she travelled up and down the Caribbean coast of Costa Rica. They lived in Limón for quite a while.

"Limón is cool, man. All the weed you want."

She has some with her. We smoke together.

The dealer got too possessive, Jessica continues, so she split. She found a place to live in the capital San José, with a woman who wanted to look after her. Until she met a Costa Rican with whom she ended up back in Nicaragua since he was running from the law in his own country. She took him to Bluefields. They had a child together. Her second kid is from that American, who dealt in tropical animals. He was supposed to take her with him to the United States, but gave up the idea when she got pregnant. And up until recently she hung out with a bunch of Colombian fishermen. They had had a real blast.

"They called me a cool-cat."

That's when her tooth got broken, she says pensively, running her right index finger over her left front tooth. An accident, too much to drink. She slipped and fell. And the fisherman, I want to know? Could they be the same Colombians who, according to the local newspaper, had been arrested for fishing illegally in Nicaraguan waters, I ask? She does not know, she says, and does not elaborate.

It is silent for a while. So I ask her about her children. They are living with her grandmother. Jessica herself is living with a friend of her mothers. And this trip? She is visiting friends.

"Anything else?"

"Not really."

She tries to stay out of all the deals going down in Bluefields as much as possible. Otherwise you'll get busted, the police turn the screws on you, you have to rat people out, scores have to be settled. There's always an errand when you take the ferry, true, but Jessica wants to have as little to do with it as possible.

"Me is a coward for that."

We get up when the room heats up too much under the sun, burning down on the zinc roof. Genoveva and her friend have already left. Jessica and I go to visit her friends. First up is Manuel, a Miskito from Prinzapolka, with whom I talk about the war years. The revolution created a lot of bad blood among the Miskitos, he says. Those living near Honduras were evacuated *en masse*. For security reasons, according to the Sandinista army, after all the *contras* were just across the border. However, many Miskito thought the Sandinistas were out to get their land and so they joined the *contras*.

Manuel tells me that the army used extreme violence against those Miskitos who refused to leave. Some of them were bound by their wrists under helicopters and cut loose high above the jungle. He himself had fled to Honduras, where he underwent military training before returning to Prinzapolka to take part in the resistance. Laying mines, going on raids, carrying out assaults.

The conflict with the Miskitos turned into the biggest blemish on the reputation of Nicaragua's revolutionary regime. There were reportedly two hundred and fifty thousand evacuees. A photograph of the charred remains of Miskito corpses became world famous. Sympathizers were troubled by the alleged violations of human rights and accusations of genocide. In turn, they were like grist to the mill of opponents of the regime. But as warily as the left talked around the subject, just as blown out of proportion were the accusations made by the right. The photograph did not show the bodies of Miskitos, but victims of Somoza's National Guard. Two hundred and fifty thousand refugees out of a total Miskito population of less than one hundred thousand were more than unlikely.

Violence died down in the course of the eighties. The ethnic groups called for greater regional autonomy in the Costa and the Sandinista regime complied. Still, Manuel is glad to be rid of the Sandinistas.

"Sandinistas, sons-of-bitches," concludes Jessica.

We have to be on our way. She has arranged to meet Nancy on the beach. I follow Jessica to Brik Bay, a small bay with a sandy beach as white as a sheet, where Nancy's mother runs a bar. After swimming the girls want their picture taken. Nancy poses like a fully fledged model. Her knees disappear under the azure blue surface of the water, she holds one hand behind her head and gracefully arches her back. She is looking for a husband, she says. There is nothing going here on the island, so couldn't I try to interest a couple of candidates with the photograph? He must be at least thirty and serious. Not necessarily rich, but somebody who has a steady job and doesn't drink. She laughs a naughty laugh and says:

"Just say I will take good care of him."

She writes down her name and address on the back of my map of the island. Nancy Wilson Terry. She is nineteen and stunning. Jessica writes down her address in Bluefields. To send her the pictures and whenever I drop by again.

Then it is time for the ladies to be off and visit other people. Apparently, my company is extraneous with Nancy around. Jessica will come and pick me up at the boarding house at six. As Nancy walks away, she hangs back. It's about her kids, she says. They need medicine, but she doesn't have enough money. I ask if fifty *córdobas* is enough. She takes it and joins her girlfriend.

I saunter along the airfield's landing strip on my way back to South West Bay. It is a long stretch of paved road that runs almost over the entire width of the island. A lot better than the dirt road full of potholes adjacent to it. Judging by the pedestrians out for a stroll, the bicyclists and the occasional motorist taking a spin on the landing strip, there won't be any planes landing for the time being.

When I reach the pier I walk on to the beach. Long, white, and almost empty.

There is a single restaurant. Except for a family having a meal under the shade of a palm tree a little further away, I am the only guest. My attention is drawn by two brawny men in their vicinity. They are keeping an eye on the family. Every once and a while they pull out walkie-talkies. Then I see that Corn Island has a prominent visitor: the father is the incumbent President of Costa Rica.

He motions to his bodyguards. They rush to him, leaning over to hear what he says, nod they have understood before using their walkie-talkies again. Not long afterwards a jeep with police officers appears. The four family members all get to their feet at the same time. The president bids a fond farewell to the restaurant owner. His lobster tasted great, if that was what it was all about. The group walks to the jeep. The bodyguards consult with the policemen. They wait. I get up and walk over. With my hand extended, I introduce myself, a little nervously. The president says it would be a great pleasure to give me an interview. Except, the plane is about to take off. He is expected in Guatemala tomorrow. But why don't I drop by and visit in San José? I am always welcome. We shake hands. The bodyguards eye me with dislike, while their boss and his family clamber into the jeep that drives off immediately.

In the shade of the palm trees I walk back to the boarding house. The late afternoon sun is still fierce. A slight breeze rustles through the branches and blows ripples across the water, that glows a yellow gold. I hear the drone of an engine. At first it fades away, and then it surges, until a small plane flies overhead. I stare at it with one hand above my eyes until it disappears in the glare of the sun. It is December 28th today. Tomorrow is the signing of an agreement in Guatemala between the government and guerillas, officially marking the end of Central America's longest civil war. Hence his departure.

The next morning a rumor is buzzing around Corn Island that the boat is coming. Are you going to look? The boat is coming. My first assumption that the *Lynx* is on its way again, proves false. It is a much bigger specimen. A cruise ship. It will reportedly drop anchor at eleven o'clock in South West Bay. I walk to the beach and see that Corn Island is getting itself ready for a grandiose reception. Cabins with thatched roofs made of palm tree leaves have appeared near the restaurant, where souvenirs are ready and waiting. T-shirts and caps with "I love Corn Island", conch shells, bracelets and necklaces, *socá*-cassettes. The cruise ship puts in at the island no more than once a month and no one should miss the chance. The passengers have dollars to spend.

A little further on a band is getting itself ready. The musicians hang around their instruments, two electric guitars, a set of bongos and an electric organ. One of them beats out a little roll, the other plucks the strings to his guitar, someone else plays a riff on the organ. A passerby cautiously tries out a few dance moves.

It is clear that *all* of Corn Island will be turning out for the fun. To the left of the restaurant is a long line of chairs, where Creole women, all dolled up in colorful dresses and wide-brimmed hats, take their places. Their husbands, most of them in their Sunday best, are standing behind them. In front of the restaurant young girls in short skirts and flowers in their hair are rehearsing their part in the welcoming ceremony. They form a double row over the beach to the waterline. The prettiest girl, arm in arm with an equally handsome boy, walk down the middle with a bouquet of flowers, which I imagine, they will hand to the captain.

From out of the restaurant Nancy walks over.

"Jessica is inside," she says.

"Why doesn't she come outside," I say tamely.

She appears a little while later. I ask her why she didn't show up yesterday.

"We went to see Nancy's mother. In the bar, you know. I had too much to drink."

She is sorry. I shrug my shoulders.

"Don't you want to come and join us?" she asks.

"Maybe later," I reply.

When she walks back, the singer asks for silence. It won't be long before the boat arrives, he says. On behalf of the entire population of the island he asks the entire population of the island to welcome the guests with open arms and to treat them well. Not to bother them, not get in people's away, not to steal.

"Remember, this is for the benefit of the community," he concludes amid loud applause.

Then he signals the band to start playing. Loud *socá* blasts over the beach. The musicians smile at one another. The crowd roars and claps. Everyone is swaying to the music.

"There she is!" a voice calls out.

The band stops playing for a moment. The women get up from their chairs. I see Jessica walk to the water line. Like everybody else she is looking towards Rocking Chair, the big cliff that separates South West Bay from the open sea. You expect to see a ship approaching from the distance. Rocking Chair is a veritable mountain, but this ship slides out from behind it as if it were just turning the corner. Suddenly it's there. Immense in its sheer presence. It sails on a bit longer and drops anchor hundreds of meters off the coastline. Nothing happens for quite a while. Jessica walks back inside. The women sit down in their chairs again.

At least an hour later a sloop is launched in the distance. It slowly approaches. Near the coast a boatswain tosses out the anchor. Small motorboats appear right away. As soon as one draws alongside, a handful of passengers disembark from the sloop, after which they are ferried ashore. One by one they are helped on land. Americans, Germans, Canadians? The pallid gentlemen with their big paunches all look the same in their blue and white naval get-ups. It is just as hard to distinguish one lady from another, with their sagging, wrinkled jowls, one hand on their floppy hat, the other on their husband's shoulders. They chirp. How exciting!

Through the lens of their whirring camcorders and clicking still cameras these ladies and gentlemen see a hedgerow of black girls in short skirts and flowers in their hair. They see black men in old-fashioned suits planted behind seated women in colorful dresses and broad-brimmed hats. And they also see – keep your distance, don't bother, don't steal – boys and girls in faded trousers and t-shirts with holes in them. Jessica is leaning against the doorpost to the restaurant. She sees the gringos pointing at the princely pair waiting with the bouquet in their arms. How cute!

But the fun doesn't last long. Once the passengers have taken enough pictures and video footage they look around, bored. Another one of those islands. The same cabins and the same knickknacks. All those people. And that music. Why the big deal? They start walking away along the water line. The girl with the flowers watches them go. The little boy has disappeared. The tourists walk to where the beach is empty. The little girl lets her bouquet droop. It doesn't look at all like the captain is going to come ashore. I walk along with the tourists, because my plane will soon be leaving for Managua. They spread their towels and plop down on the sand, gasping.

At the bar near the airport Alan and Sharon greet me with delight. They offer me a farewell drink. They will be staying on for a couple more days. Sharon knows for sure that I will come back.

That much is certain, once you have been here. I ask Alan when he plans to relocate back to Bluefields. He says sooner rather than later, but you don't want to rush into anything.

"Let's hope peace will last and our country can grow to be mature."

Sharon hopes especially that their region will receive some more attention. As an inhabitant of the Costa she is all too familiar with the arrogance of the Pacífico. Alan can understand why some think that regional autonomy does not go far enough. If the government fails to do anything for you, then there comes a time when you decide to take care of your own affairs. Sharon, however, does not believe in an independent Costa.

"We are condemned to the Pacífico," she says.

"And they to us," Allan rejoins.

As I am sitting in the plane strapped into my safety belt, Alan rushes onto the runway. The shrieking propellers blow his hair around. He is holding up a pair of sunglasses. I motion they are not mine. We wave to one another. The plane accelerates and starts rushing towards the Caribbean Sea. Above the water, the pilot turns the plane a hundred and eighty degrees and sets course over the island towards the mainland. The runway lies below. Alan is not there anymore. If you were to raise the problems in the Costa to a global scale, he thought, then the solution to the world's issues lay in the mixing of the races. "Once there are no more pure bred races left, no one will feel superior to the other," he said.

The cruisers down below are lying like dollops of vanilla pudding along the beach. I hope that, somewhere in between their sunbathing, they have managed to find the strength to still buy up all the knickknacks and eat all the lobster and drink all the beer. For the benefit of the community.

And Jessica? If she has heard the droning of the engine, then maybe she is now standing on the beach with a hand cupped above her eyes staring at the little plane until it has become a black dot, disappearing in the glare of the sun.

BACK to MANAGUA

THE MAGDALENA II

Around midday doña Aura climbs the short flight of stairs onto the porch. She leans against the railing to catch her breath. Since her fall she has hardly been at Magdalena. For more than a month now. Today, however, her presence is mandatory. The general assembly is meeting and all members of the cooperative have to attend. Her hand is no longer swollen, but it still hurts, especially the middle part of it.

"What did the doctor have to say?"

She grimaces at me with fear. No way is she going to see a doctor!

"What if they cut me open?"

I ask how her Easter was. Quiet, says Aura. Nothing happened, like the way it ought to be.

"They were fine days with Jesus."

Aura has been working at Magdalena ever since she was a girl. There were always quite a few people coming and going when the Velázquez family lived there. They had lain a stone path all the way to Balgüe, down which the carts laden with coffee drove. Here and there in the yard are some of the original cobblestones from that old path.

"Where are the rest of them?" I enquire.

She looks at me with surprise.

"When nobody bothers to look at them?"

The Velázquez's were honest people, she continues, though you didn't make much, two or three pesos a day. But back then a pound of rice only cost eighty cents. The family lived upstairs. In the room where I'm staying, the lady of the house used to run a store. "The rat" they called her, laughs Aura. The oranges were stored in what are now the sleeping quarters. Today, no oranges are left. That is because the Baltodanos let the orange trees dry out. They came at the end of the sixties, when the Velázquez's could no longer pay off their debts. After the 1979 revolution the Baltodanos fled to the United States. On the *finca* overseers were left behind with orders to decapitalize the business. All the cattle was sold, the household furniture, the machinery. The confiscation must have taken place at the beginning of the eighties.

"Didn't the Sandinistas only confiscate Somoza's properties?" I ask.

"Sure enough, but the Baltdono's were miniature Somoza's. There was even a marriage brewing with one of Somoza's sons."

Aura points to the field in front of the of farm entrance, where Somoza's helicopter always landed. It used to be full of *guardias*.

"The Baltodano's have filed a lawsuit against us," says Aura. "They want the *finca* back. "But," she adds, "we are going to defend ourselves."

"How? With weapons?"

"No," she laughs. "With papers."

We walk into the storeroom. Aura sits at her table. She can understand why Yadira wants to go to Costa Rica. Her own daughter has been working there for more than two years now. That family treats her like one of their own children. She takes her meals with them at the same table, has her own room with a shower, toilet and television and only has to prepare one meal a day. In Nicaraguan currency, that comes to sixteen hundred *córdobas* a month. You ought to see what it is here. Recently, a store was looking for hired help. For five *córdobas* a day! Who is going to work for that? If you ask Aura, that's just the way this country is. If people around here don't change the way they behave, things will never change. Who still cares about the farmers? For them it is a daily struggle to survive.

She too went away in the past, two years to Granada and two years to Managua. Before the earthquake, it used to be a beautiful city, but even then you heard rumors of an impending war and that is why she came back. She picks at her hand. This year she would not be able to do much on her plot of land on the plantation. Then she rearranges her bookkeeping ledgers and says that she anyhow prefers keeping the books and selling drinks. But if she has to, she will go and work on the land. Women already do the same work as the men do.

"Except that we don't swing these machetes around like them."

She does not need a husband anymore. One year after the birth of Mauricio, her youngest, she put her man out of the house. There are a lot of single mothers in Balgüe, I remark. Aura gives me a roguish look.

"Single? That's because you only see them during the day."

She herself? No, she is alone at night too. But she doesn't complain. Why would she?

"I am a child of the King."

Her faith in God takes precedence over everything else. Doesn't it say in the Bible that the Son has come to save us?

"And what about the farm? Aren't you all grateful to the Lord for the Magdalena? I don't think many farmers in Nicaragua have as much land as you do."

"This land does not belong to us at all."

"How's that?"

"And if they take it away from us?"

"But the land is yours now, isn't it?"

Doña Aura smiles at me benignly.

"Yes, but you never know."

She is silent, engrossed in reflection.

"Take this year's coffee harvest, for instance," she continues. "It's April now. You were here yourself back in January, when all the women were doing the threshing, weren't you? We were finished in February, but the coffee still hasn't been sold."

Yadira comes in. She tells how busy it has been during Easter. There were at least thirty guests. Tiring. But in another two weeks it will all be done, then she will be leaving. She smiles, without a handkerchief, even though her front teeth are still missing.

I announce that my boxing match is set for mid-May. Which is why I won't be staying very long, either. The next month I want to train in Managua.

"Are you going to Costa Rica, right away?" I ask Yadira.

"No, first my teeth."

They will be ready at the beginning of May. Four of them, including two crowns, all totaled, six hundred *córdobas*.

"You couldn't get a single tooth for that price where I come from," I tell her.

"But you guys don't make four hundred and fifty *córdobas* a month."

I gather from this that she has been saving up since January and has been without front teeth all that time. I keep the thought to myself though.

"And the farmers, where are they?"

"At home. They took Easter off. Tomorrow is their first working day back."

Yadira still has to see who will be coming. They are busy with their own land. There is little time left for the cooperative. Luckily, tourism is doing well, because as long as the coffee has not been sold, they have no other income. Almost every cent made with tourism pays the costs incurred by agricultural activities.

"As if we didn't have to buy supplies," Yadira sighs.

Through the door, I see a woman approaching with a blue plastic tub on her head. She carefully sets it down on the table. Once seated, she daubs the sweat from her brow with a towel. She comes here every other day, says doña Aura, from Las Cuchillas, a village about an hour away on foot. Later, she'll continue on to Balgüe and then go back to her village.

"I've got eggs. Do you want some, girl?" she asks Yadira, who is standing in the doorway now.

Yadira has a look and buys them all.

"And bananas?" the woman asks.

Yadira says no. She bought them last time, there are still plenty left.

The woman again wipes the sweat from her forehead, she puts the towel on her head and the tub on top of that. She says goodbye while getting to her feet. Cautiously, she goes down the steps to the exit, and heads towards the path that leads to Balgüe.

"How come you buy bananas?" I ask Yadira when the woman has disappeared from sight. "Every famer grows their own, don't they?"

"That is meant for home use," she answers, "not for here."

Bananas, rice, beans, the farmers grow everything, she continues, but it's been years since they did so collectively. The storehouse always used to be full and the farmers divided the harvest among themselves. The cooperative has also lost so much land. Of the twelve hundred *manzanas* from the early days, only five hundred are left and most of that is for private use. On top of that, land is being leased.

"But now they could feed it to the tourists," I suggest, "that would cut down on the cost of buying supplies."

"H'm," Yadira agrees, "but nobody feels like doing it."

Blanca and Juan have gone to visit Blanca's mother on the coast during Easter. Juan is gasping for breath after the climb out of Balgüe. He runs a comb through his hair and says that the vacation has actually lasted too long. You can only leave a farm alone for a few days at most.

"Be careful," I tease him, "otherwise no other farmers will show up."

"They'd better," he replies, "today is the general assembly."

But Juan is far from satisfied.

"Get a load of this roof," he says looking up, "it leaks like a sieve. Do you think anybody has bothered to fix it?"

He gives me a serious look.

"Do you know what it is? Too many people here are used to taking orders. Do this, do that."

The Magdalena has a lot of good land, he says, you must be a real idiot to die of hunger here. But the people do not know the true value of the land. They figure I have enough to eat today, and that's that. And they keep on making the same mistakes, over and over.

"That's the way we always used to do it, you then hear, so why should we do it any different now?"

"But, a lot of you can still remember how it was under the Baltadano's, right?"

"Most of us. You were exploited. You got four hour's pay for eight hours of work."

He laughs.

"Now it's the other way around: we work four hours and pay ourselves for eight."

Juan is not surprised that Yadira is leaving. She works like crazy, sometimes until eleven at night. And what kind of money does she make?

People around here don't encourage one another. It's rather the opposite. If you do your best, they say you are stealing from them. Instead of them trying to do their best too. Maybe, he ought to do more for himself, Juan muses, like cattle breeding, that doesn't require a lot of investment and can pay quite well. Leave? Never. He will not run out on his *compañeros*.

At three o'clock Feliciano summons all members to gather for the assembly. Everybody goes upstairs. The meeting will be held in the dormer.

When I pass by underneath around five o'clock, I can hear the meeting is still going on. One of the men beckons me to come upstairs. Everyone is sitting is a semi-circle in front of chairman Feliciano's table. Bernabé is reading a letter from one of the cooperative's foreign members, who sends his congratulations for such a good coffee harvest.

And Bernabé has news. He takes off his reading glasses and eyes his audience with satisfaction.

"The transportation has been arranged," he says, "the coffee is going to be shipped."

There are murmurs of assent, sounds of laughter and handshakes all around. Finally!

"I would like to proceed," says Feliciano, waiting until silence is restored.

At first he beams a smile at everyone, which does not appear to come readily. Then, staring seriously at the floor in the midst of everyone, he announces his decision to resign his office as chairman. The new chairman Felix is sitting next to him, he says. In closing this assembly, Feliciano would like to pass on the administration of the cooperation to him. He takes up the charter book and gives it to Felix, followed by the journal, the memorandum of association and the deed of transfer. He holds one document empathetically aloft for all to see.

"This is the title to ownership," he says. "Before transferring this, I invite everyone present to come and inspect it."

He lays the document on the table. Four members get to their feet and toss a cursory glance at the piece of paper and sit back down. Then Feliciano slides it over to Felix.

"And finally, I transfer Sandino," says Feliciano.

He shows everyone a portrait of the freedom fighter.

"Long live Sandino," resounds.

"The guy's been dead for years," somebody jokes.

"But he lives on in our hearts," another one softly says.

The next day the burlap bags have arrived. Now the coffee beans can be tipped from the orange plastic sacks into the burlap bags, on which the following text should be printed: *Premium Organic Coffee, produced by cooperative Carlos Díaz Cajína, Island of Ometepe, Nicaragua,* with the Magdalena logo on top. It takes ninety-six bags to fill a total harvest of nearly seven thousand kilos.

Bernabé comes to sit next to me on the porch. He has been in Granada for days to arrange the shipment. There has been a two month delay, that is nothing to sneeze at, but they have managed, and that is what counts. The cooperative has always faced obstacles. It all began after it had started to crumble. Initially the cooperative had been a lot bigger, but it fell apart because many members did not rally behind the collective. The first few years, there was a favorable climate for agriculture though. The banks extended soft loans. You received technical assistance. Now market thinking has become dominant. New loans have become more expensive and the old ones reassessed. There was one year in which Magdalena's debt more than tripled. Especially when you take into account that nobody actually had the slightest inkling of how to run a business, it is not surprising that the cooperative has had to steer through rough waters.

"We were simple day laborers," says Bernabé. "We were not prepared to have to manage commodities."

Bernabé himself does believe in the cooperative as an organizational form. Together you are strong. Even though being together can also be a weakness. In the end, not everyone is equal and how do you get minds and energy moving in the same direction? But if you compare it to the *fincas* now operating on an individual basis, you can see it is not the collective that can be blamed for the lack of progress made over all those years. It has to do with the means at your disposal and the knowledge of what to do with them.

"Imagine you are a boxer and you want to prepare for a fight, but you have no money and no one wants to give you an advance. How can you go and fight then?"

And yet: the cooperative exists. The people at Magdalena are fully aware of just how exceptional that is. Not that Bernabé feels that the farmers are not entitled to this property. On the contrary. After all, they are the ones who have always worked the land. But a revolutionary process like that of sandinism, of which Magdalena is a consequence, will perhaps never reoccur. Many farmers have not fully assessed the value of its achievements and are back to where they were before the Revolution. Bernabé is of the opinion that the Magdalena has an obligation. As a collective. You stand together, no matter how different one is from the other. You carry on, in good times and in bad.

"A marriage?" I ask.

It makes us both laugh, but Bernabé gives me a serious answer. "Yes, you are married to the cooperative."

I hear heehawing behind me. I turn around and see the donkeys, all eight of them. They have been fitted out with wooden frames. Two men walk up to the donkeys, each with a bale of coffee on his shoulder. They go and stand on either side of the donkey and toss their bale on the frame. Then one man straps a rope underneath and pulls it tight. Two bales per donkey, sixteen per caravan. Poor donkeys, there they go, out of the yard, their hooves clattering on the stones. A stubborn beast who walks off the track, gets the whip. Ninety-six bales: six times back and forth to Balgüe. All today, because tomorrow morning early the whole cargo has to be taken by truck to the harbor at Altagracia. The boat to Granada departs at ten.

I walk upstairs and go and sit next to Feliciano on the window sill of the dormer. A burden has fallen from his shoulders, he says. As chairman everybody always have their eye on you. Take Blanca. She tells him it's his fault that somebody else has been appointed to work in the kitchen, whereas the decision had been taken collectively by all the members. And whenever you put your finger on a problem, you always get flack. Under the Baltodano's there was no work for you if you did not show up at six. If you say anything about it now, all you hear is: "he thinks he can lay down the law as if we were still living back then." People are thinking too much about themselves. The same thing happened when the land was redistributed. It's all very well and good to say: "let's all fight to keep the land together," but if the majority does not want to, it won't help.

"We call ourselves a cooperative", says Feliciano sourly, "but if the co-op asks something, we are not there for it. On the other hand, if the cooperative has something to give, all of a sudden everyone is at the front of the line."

The past few months have been exceptionally hard. He had started to have serious doubts about himself and wondered whether or not he was letting Magdalena go down the tubes. It has made him ill. And yet Feliciano does not look back without satisfaction. Which chairman is able to say that he left the cooperation flush with money? When he took office there were no cash funds.

"Did you know that even the title to ownership wasn't there?"

The document turned out to be at one of the member's homes. Feliciano thanks God he was able to successfully lay a hand on it. A man must be humble.

"I beseeched Him for help and He gave me the insight."

According to Feliciano, that other person had had his plan. That of being able to fight if anyone would come to claim the *finca*, like the Baltodanos were now doing.

"But Magdalena belongs to all of us. We have to fight as one."

So he had had his reasons for bringing the document to everyone's attention so empathetically the day before.

"And did you notice how few of them had a look," he asks disappointedly.

"And Sandino?" I enquire.

"He is depicted on the cover to the papers which farmers received when the Sandinistas allocated land to them in accordance with the Land Reform Act."

"So, it's a gift of history, this cooperative."

There is a serious look in Feliciano's eyes.

"Sandino gave his life, so that us farmers could own the land. That is the legacy we bear."

At the end of the afternoon, the donkeys leave the yard for the last time. Once the coffee has arrived at Granada it will go by truck to the harbor at Corinto on the Pacific Coast, where the cargo will be shipped to Canada.

The last donkey disappears behind the trees. The contours of the canopy, through which the majestic crown of a kapok tree towers here and there, are hazy. That is because of the smoke which has been hanging above Ometepe for weeks. The dry season is drawing to a close and the farmers set fire to their land to rid it of old planting and weeds before the rains come. One day the wind drove the fire close to Magdalena. A great many buckets of water were needed to save the *finca* from the flames.

The sinking sun shines gloomily through the blanket of smoke. It is as if you are looking at a sepia photograph of an unreal landscape shrouded in hues of gray and orange. The orange shading even deeper than usual, almost the color of blood. The lake in the distance is gray, the coastline vague, the peninsula behind which the bay at Santo Domingo begins, a shadow. Beyond the bay, further away, lies the Concepción, immense, dark and orange. Wouldn't Yadira miss this view? Would she be able to receive radio Tigre in Costa Rica?

Feliciano has gone home. Just before he left, I had made a grand gesture with my arms and said: "All you survey is yours."

"When you consider that we wound up here...," Feliciano had sighed, followed by a grin from ear to ear.

"Magdalena is a gift from God."

THE MATCH II

"And my sardine?"

I give Vampiro a questioning look. Didn't I know you were supposed to treat your trainer to a sardine for Easter, he asks?

"It doesn't matter, doesn't matter. You're a foreigner, just like me. It will come. Change your clothes *Tulipán*. Get a move on."

Things are serious now. On Tuesday, during the weekly meeting of trainers in the *Alexis*, Vampiro arranged a match. I'm fighting on May 15th. We are obligated now. He shrugs off my concerns with a wave of his hand. That slight case of the flu I had last week is over, isn't it? Now that I am back in Managua, I just have to train every day, including Saturday. We still have more than a month. Plenty of time. It is not a professional bout! He has worked everything out. Jumping rope is up first.

"Fifteen minutes. Come on Tulipán."

The nickname has been born out of necessity. To keep from being called gringo or German all the time. Vampiro is over the moon.

"Tu-li-pán!" resounds through the hall. "Ok, that's enough. Hand wraps on and shadowbox, two rounds. Hurry up."

He follows my every move.

"Your hips, *Tuli*, move them, salsa! I want to see that left jab, faster. Wallop that guy. *Con clase,* Tulipán, four punches, move around fast and with class!"

118

Vampiro is not dissatisfied, but of course I'm never going to amount to much.

"It's not for nothing they say that boxing is for blacks. A black man is faster, smarter and stronger. Just try and lay a hand on me."

He drops his hands and moves his upper body. Left, ducks, to the right. I can't get near him.

"You see," he laughs. "I was quicker than all these guys around here put together."

He puts on focus mitts and holds them up.

"Left, Tuli, left, move, left-right, on the mitts, faster, Tuli, left and turn, four jabs, one-two-three-four. Dance, Dutchman. *Boxear.* Everything at once."

He takes off the mitts and puts up his dukes.

"Just watch me. Move and punch. Left, uppercut, hook, right and turn away, tease, left, left, left, move, your feet, your waist, left, right, go down, uppercut, uppercut and move again."

I am stunned by his speed and agility.

"Boxing is a profession, Dutchman. An art."

From the corner of his eye he looks at Rodrigo, who is at work on the bag.

"I never show these kinds of things to anyone."

He leans over to me.

"You know what it is. They drop you like a stone. You train them and teach them everything and then they go and look for someone else who takes all the credit. No pal, this black man is keeping his mouth shut."

After the training session we have a coke around the corner near the stadium. They are looking for a rookie to face me, Vampiro says. Is it really true I have never been in a boxing match? He has told everyone that I started boxing with him, six months earlier.

"I can't look like a chump," Vampiro says underscoring the importance of our obligation. "You and me are foreigners. They all want to see us lose."

There is one thing I must promise him, that I will not run off to someone else. I will not, I tell him, provided he treats me right.

"But that's just the point. The better you treat them the sooner they leave."

"Where to? I just want to fight once. This will be both my debut and farewell."

"I wouldn't say that just yet, Tulipán. Boxing gets in your blood."

"By the way," I continue, "two weeks after the fight I am going back home."

He looks at me with surprise. Then I have to arrange something there for him. Once they have seen me box, they will say: "Bring that black guy over here to train." Or haven't I learned a helluva lot from him already? Sure enough, I admit. He doesn't have to worry about a thing. I won't go to someone else.

"You have to fight like it's the last thing you do in life, Tulipán. We have to win this bout."

When I leave I gave him twice his fee.

"For the sardine."

He looks wide-eyed at the banknotes in his hand.

"How am I supposed to eat sardines on this?"

I show him my empty wallet.

"And what I am supposed to eat with this?"

I am standing near the entrance to the arena, waiting for Vampiro. Burro comes outside. He starts talking about a priest who boxes. In my weight class. That would really be something. But, you couldn't really hit him of course, otherwise you'd get into trouble in heaven. He chuckles at himself. He thinks I'm slow, and all those questions to Vampiro, am I going to do that in the ring too? Burro, I say, Burro, do you know what that means? Donkey. Empty-headed. And you can't win a fight with an empty head.

Vampiro comes over. What does he think of the priest, Burro asks. Are you nuts, says Vampiro, he's been around for years. No, the Dutchman is going up against a rookie, some middle-class type, which is just as well because they fight not because they have to. That guy has already been training for two years, but hey, no, not that priest, no way.

Vampiro has to fetch something inside and then we can go. Burro turns his nose up at him as he goes.

"Watch your step. If you're unlucky that middle-class kid will already have thirty bouts under his belt."

He spits on the ground.

"That's the way it works. Matches are sold. Everybody is in for a piece of the action."

The ring in the middle of the *Alexis* is empty, just like the four stands, one against each wall, which I estimate could hold about four hundred people. Training is going on in every corner. Shoulder to shoulder young boys on three by four meter wooden pallets are jumping rope. Vampiro walks ahead of me into the locker room, where the weigh-in scales are, the best in Managua, he says. He adjusts the scales to my weight and motions me to stand on it. When the indicator stops swinging back and forth, he nods, everything's in order.

Back in the arena Vampiro introduces me to Guillermo *Polvorita* Martínez, my opponent's trainer. He sizes me up slowly from head to toe and grudgingly tells me the name of my opponent, Silvio.

When we leave the building, Vampiro clicks his tongue with disapproval.

"There are at least seven trainers working here. Those guys can't stand one another. They all work against each other, they have their eyes on each other's talents."

I tell him I don't want to have a thing to do with any of that. I have one trainer, and that is him. But I do want to be able to trust him. He is wide-eyed with surprise. Don't I get it, that he is a foreigner, just like me? All those dudes over there want to drink his blood. But he has earned his place. He was Vampiro Meléndez and nobody can take that away from him. Did I think some Nicaraguan trainer was going to make me win? With Burro? Never. He had been talking to me, hadn't he? That the match had been fixed and such stuff. That Burro just can't stand having lost that foreigner.

"A bunch of brutes, all of them," he cries.

He must have been around twenty, when he had asked one of those intellectual types where in Central America people were the crudest and that man had answered in Nicaragua. "Then, that is where I'm going," he had said in reply.

We are back in the stadium. Vampiro goes to sit on his desk.

"Well, I kept my word," he laughs. "I have been living here for twenty-six years now."

But Panamanians are smarter. Because Panama is not Central American, nor is it South American. Vampiro gets to his feet. Panama, he says, is the center, the heart of the universe! His country has been independent ever since 1903, separated from Colombia. Everything around here used to belong to Mexico.

The year before, when he had been training Tomas Borge, he had asked him: "Jefe, how have things come to this?" And what did Borge say? It was because Nicaraguans were such brutes. He could not believe his ears. But you can't fool him. He has been in eighteen different countries. He boxed as far away as Japan. And he has faced combat. Here, in the mountains and later in the army. Colonel Vampiro. And all the women he has had. In Costa Rica, for instance. Twenty-four, twenty-five, he was. He had a girl on the coast. Dropped her off at four o'clock in the afternoon to go to work and picked her up at eleven to settle accounts. Then a meal, a drink and hit the sack. Screw. What a life! He looks up, that was what he was most proud of, all those women. He looks down again and then at me.

"I fucked, fought, killed, was taken prisoner, had money, clothes, women, everything!"

He bangs the desktop with the palm of his hand. "Is that good, or what?"

"Tu-li-pán!"

Gustavo walks in, grinning from ear to ear. Too late to spar, because I am already sweating it out. Vampiro thinks I should train with him and not with Rodrigo, who prances around the arena like some untamed lion.

"He wants to show how hard he can hit," says Vampiro. "That won't do you any good. You can learn from Gustavo."

Gustavo has still not got any reaction from Miami after that phone call last week. An old friend of his. If he wanted to come and box. He would go at the drop of a hat, he says. At twenty-nine he has no more time to lose. And boxing in Nicaragua… ah, I had seen the *Alexis* with my own eyes, hadn't I? What good would that do?

"Tulipán," he says again.

"Haven't you got a nickname?"

"The name's Herrera. Gustavo Herrera. That is my real name. Otherwise, people only know you by your nickname. Now they say: "Hey, there goes Herrera.""

He could have had it made for life, they say. But hey, a sportsman can't change politics. You were not allowed to make any money under the Sandinistas. On the other hand, he was on the government payroll. The best paid sportsman in Nicaragua. And apart from that, he was Gustavo Herrera. He could do whatever he liked and go where ever he wanted, with or without money. Well, maybe he should have hawked his talent in a better way. There had been plenty of offers. From Venezuela, Mexico. If only he had been single at the time. But he fell in love with a student. They are still together. Isn't that more important than money?

Vampiro motions to me. Go ahead and spar with Rodrigo anyway, he says. After all, we will practically be boxing at the same time, his match is scheduled the day after mine. There is a frightful grin on Rodrigo's face and he lets himself be goaded into cutting this foreigner down to size. Vampiro orders us to take it easy, he looks at his watch and signals for us to begin.

Rodrigo, who is shorter than I am, tries to fight up close with punches to the ribs, but I keep him at a distance with my left hand. I get through a couple of times when he lets his guard down. I throw a combination of a direct left followed by a hook, but too slowly. Rodrigo responds with a right hook to the chin. After two rounds I am out of breath.

"You're improving," says Vampiro to my astonishment.

They have put him under pressure at the *Alexis*, Vampiro tells me the next day.

"They've already heard about those punches yesterday," he says looking to the other corner of the arena, where Burro is smoking a cigarette.

Let that foreigner throw the fight. He wasn't going to let his colleagues down, right? This guy is my bread and butter ticket, he answered. And what good are any of you to me? None whatsoever. Then Vampiro says that Polvorita has pulled Silvio out. "You're going to win because they are scared," my neighbor Mario once told me. There are two other candidates. Polvorita has Parrales, an experienced fighter, and trainer Mena has a rookie named Aguirre. No way, says Rodrigo, who is standing next to us. Aguirre has a least twenty fights to his name. Then it had better be Parrales, concludes Vampiro. By the way, he says sternly, what difference does it really make who it is? What's all this whining about? He had made his professional debut against the champion of Panama. He had only been in the ring three times before that and never more than three rounds. That match was to go twelve full rounds.

"And?" I ask.

"I won."

He wanders back into the arena singing a tune with a satisfied grin on his face. "*Tanto tiempo disfrutando...pa, pa, pa.*"

Vampiro has done the definite deal. Exactly a week from now. Opponent: Marvin Aguilar Aguirre. Parrales turned out to be much too experienced, he has over thirty fights to his name. Vampiro saw Aguirre yesterday.

"'I'm going to eat that foreigner raw,' he said," sneers Vampiro. "But don't you worry, Aguirre's a lush."

I spar with a pupil of Burro's and get chewed out when I'm done.

"How could you let him come like that!" Vampiro roars. "You're the one calling the shots, Dutchman!"

"*Adornar,* they say in Cuba," Gustavo rejoins, "decorate, keep your opponent busy, don't give him any time to think."

Gustavo and I sit down. He wants to know why I started boxing. And what has made me want to fight a match here? I keep silent about wanting to write about it. I'm saving that for Vampiro. I have told him that I owed him a story, about the mysterious boxer from Holland. Vampiro had looked at me disgruntled, saying "what the hell are you talking about?" I would explain it to him before I left. To Gustavo I say that I have once been attacked by a group of five boys and was barely able to defend myself. And that I had started boxing after that.

"There is always a reason," he says.

Gustavo tells me how as a little boy, he went to see his dad box, who used to fight for a living. One time a younger boxer had knocked him senseless and he woke up in the hospital. Gustavo started boxing so he could beat that man some day.

"And?"

"It never happened."

But Gustavo Herrera did become one of Nicaragua's best boxers of the nineteen eighties. He reached number three on the world lightweight rankings. He went to Cuba twenty-five times for training camps. Felix Savón, Cuba's famous heavyweight, is an old buddy of his, and no Nicaraguan boxer has more victories over a Cuban than him.

Our attention is drawn by Vampiro standing near his desk, shouting.

"I shit on the mother of Satan!"

No idea what he is talking about.

"Satan is a fallen angel, Vampiro," I say. "So that means you are actually shitting on God's wife."

He frowns.

"Don't they say he dwells in purgatory?"

"In the deepest ring of all."

His face brightens.

"Then it's ok! Satan is evil incarnate, you see. And that's just how life is, you have good and you have evil and without good and evil there is no life."

The final training session is over. I am packing up my stuff and listen to Vampiro's advice for tomorrow. Rest, is his motto. First have a hearty breakfast, then on to the *Alexis* for the weighing in. Go back home and watch some television, read a book, take a nap. Have a light meal at four, a sandwich and a cup of tea and back to the *Alexis*. The matches start at six.

He thinks having a massage is a good idea, but it should be today, you don't do something like that on the day of a fight. I toss my kit bag over my shoulder and head for the exit. Vampiro slides off his desktop and strolls into the arena.

"*Pa, pa, pa, …tanto tiempo.*"

I turn around.

"Vampiro?"

He looks over his shoulder.

"What's that song you keep singing?"

He grins.

"It's an old tune. From Panama."

"What's it about?"

"It's about, how shall I put it, it's just about how a guy is enjoying the way his girl is loving him."

There is a melancholy look in his eye.

"She made it up about Vampiro," he finally says. "Because I was so dark, she said."

"Can you sing it for me?"

He shakes his head, giggling.

"Tulipán! Take it easy, man."

I insist. At first he glances at me hesitantly, then turns his head and starts singing softly:

> "*Tanto tiempo disfrutando de este amor,*
> *nuestras almas se acercaron tanto así…*
> *pa, pa, pa…*"
> (Having enjoyed that love for so long,
> our souls came so close to one another)

"Something like that," he says and walks away.

My neighbor Alicia's grandmother is already waiting for me. We shuffle to the massage parlor, two streets away. Doing massages actually began out of necessity, she tells me while unpacking her gear. She had to make a living somehow after her husband ran out on her ten years ago.

I am told to lay down on the table, close my eyes and take a couple of deep breaths.

"So," she says, "now all I want you to do is think about tomorrow's match, and that you will come out a winner."

Her fingers slowly slide downward over my arm. She presses gently, kneads, holds my hand and shakes. I hear her walking around the table. She starts on the other arm.

The match has been on my mind constantly the last few weeks. Three rounds of three minutes. That is all you get. I see the narrow path running through the banana fields on Ometepe. Down the slope at first, stretching exercises in the village and back up the mountain, day in, day out, for five months. Then the strength training in my room at the back of Magdalena and working on the corn bag. The training with Vampiro would start with fifteen minutes of jumping rope. Next came the drills, four minutes long with a minute's rest. Move. Feet. Hips. Decorate. How can you make sure that your strength, technique and insights are all set? Keep your distance. Left, left, left. Wallop that guy. How to deal with the unexpected and react to it in a split second? One, two, three, four and turn away, out of that hell. How do you control the fear of the other without losing the agility required to break down his defenses? *Boxear*. Everything at once. How do you do that, get "mentally prepared?" Are you supposed to hate your opponent and take out your anger on him? But I don't even know the guy, that Marvin. The whole neighborhood is on my side, said Mario, my neighbor. My match was their match. That's why I should not let myself be beaten up. But I do not want to win out of fear of losing. Tomorrow they will turn on the radio at Magdalena to listen to coverage of the boxing match. A lot of Dutch people will be there to watch, even the ambassadress considered it. Of course, I want to win for them. But was it that what got it started in the first place? The question is why I actually want to fight. Two years ago, I went to Latin America to write a series of articles. The book came as a result of it. I had not anticipated having a boxing match. I am fighting to write a story about it. And it ends tomorrow. The match, I realize, is the end. The end of the story.

I may open my eyes again and am told to slowly exhale.

"To finish up we are going to remove all the negativity in you," says grandma.

She wipes her hands down over my arms and legs and then shakes them, getting rid of imaginary dust.

Vampiro is already waiting for me, when I arrive at the *Alexis* the next morning at eight. It's crowded around the scales. When it's my turn, the inspector adjusts them to eighty-one kilos, my match weight. The pointers tip. The inspector asks me to get off for a moment and readjusts the weight. Now the pointers are in balance. Eighty-two point eight. Nearly two kilos too much! I protest. That's impossible. I weighed myself only yesterday. I look at Vampiro, saying someone has tampered with that thing. There's a menacing glint in Vampiro's eyes.

"No way. This is the official pair of scales."

He grabs me by the arm.

"You're allowed to be one kilo overweight. The weighing goes on until nine o'clock. What are you waiting for!"

He paces in front of me to a cramped space under the stands, snatches a rope from the wall and hands it to me.

"Start jumping!"

Vampiro hands me a plastic training shirt.

"Put it on. Sweat."

He comes back twenty minutes later.

"That's enough. Back to the scales."

Dripping with perspiration, I step on the scales, tense. Don't move, says the inspector. The pointer swings back and forth before coming to a stop. At exactly eighty-two kilos!

"In order," says the inspector, putting a check to my name on his list.

Vampiro laughs.

"Fluid, Tulipán. You drank too much water."

Finally, I can go outside for a breath of fresh air. At the door however, I am held back by a man looking at me with a sad expression on his face.

"He went out for a run this morning and that's when he fell on his wrist," he says.

I do not understand what the man is talking about. Vampiro asks what is going on. I repeat what I have just heard. He swears.

"Who is this?" I ask.

"Mena."

Mena looks even sadder now.

"I can't help it either."

I walk back into the arena. Vampiro comes after me.

"There is not a boxer in the world who goes out for a run on the day of a fight," he snorts. "If he fell on anything, it was his balls."

Vampiro is called away. He starts discussing with a group of men, he gesticulates, pats them on the shoulders before coming back to me.

"Listen, you know that boxing is all fixed."

He turns his head toward the group of men.

"We can arrange another opponent for you. For two hundred *córdobas.* They'll find somebody. Some palooka."

I say I will think about it and walk over to the ring. Up a short flight of steps I clamber through the ropes. The canvas gives in a little, there is probably foam rubber underneath. A circular shaped depiction of two boxers has been affixed to the middle of the ring. The ropes are thick and give way when you hang in them. I climb back down the stairs and sit in the stands. Vampiro comes and sits next to me.

"I'm not going to do it," I say.

He nods.

"What have I been telling you?" he finally says. "They can't be trusted."

Stoical, he stares into space.

"I fought for this country. I gave up my passport for it. And look...all I can do is resign myself to it."

I think of the story I was going to tell him. The story about the mysterious boxer from Holland. I am going to tell you the story of the match that never became a match, Vampiro. It's called "The Match."

GLOSSARY

Balsero – the term used for Cubans that left their country by raft

Burro – donkey

Caballería – old Spanish unit of square area, approximately 45 hectares

Cacique – chief, local ruler or leader

Casa de los Leones – House of the Lions

Club Social – meeting place for the well-to-do

Conquista – the conquest, namely the Spanish conquest of Latin America

Conquistador – conqueror

Córboda – the Nicaraguan unit of currency

Costeño – coastal inhabitant

Creole – someone of African descent, descendants of slaves, a black person

Criollo – someone born in Latin America of European descent, not to be confused with creole

Curandero – healer, curer

Finca – farm, land estate

Frente – Front, short for the Sandinista Front for National Liberation

FSLN – abbreviation of the Sandinista Front for National Liberation

Genízaro – tropical species of tree

Guardia – guard, specially the name of a member of Somoza's National Guard

Guerillero – guerilla fighter

Jefe – chief, leader

Manzana – unit of square area, approx. 0.7 hectares

Mestizo – someone of Amerindian and white (criollo) descent

Morena – black woman

Socá – dance from the Caribbean region of Nicaragua

Tulipán – tulip

Urraca – blue-white feathered magpie

ACKNOWLEDGEMENTS

The story "The Children of Adiact" appeared in an amended, journalistic version in *Revista Latina*, no. 26, 1997, with the title "De koninklijke rechten van Subtiava".

The story "Faith" appeared in July 1997 in the Nicaraguan newspaper *La Tribuna* with the title of "No hay fe."

The name of some of the characters in this book has been changed for privacy reasons.

All Spanish language excerpts appearing in the book were originally translated into Dutch by the author, except for the quote by Julio Cortazar in the opening story.

My thanks go out to all those whose stories are included here; a world of thanks also to Alicia Zamora for all her information, and I would like to extend a special word of gratitude to Jeroen Neumann for his uncompromising comments with regard to style.

Printed in the United States
By Bookmasters